Social Research Perspectives

Occasional Reports on Current Topics

13

Inspectors-General

Junkyard Dogs or Man's Best Friend?

by Mark H. Moore and
Margaret Jane Gates

RUSSELL SAGE FOUNDATION   NEW YORK

The Russell Sage Foundation

The Russell Sage Foundation, one of the oldest of America's general purpose foundations, was established in 1907 by Mrs. Margaret Olivia Sage for "the improvement of social and living conditions in the United States." The Foundation seeks to fulfill this mandate by fostering the development and dissemination of knowledge about the political, social, and economic problems of America. It conducts research in the social sciences and public policy, and publishes books and pamphlets that derive from this research.

The Board of Trustees is responsible for oversight and the general policies of the Foundation, while administrative direction of the program and staff is vested in the President, assisted by the officers and staff. The President bears final responsibility for the decision to publish a manuscript as a Russell Sage Foundation book. In reaching a judgement on the competence, accuracy, and objectivity of each study, the President is advised by the staff and selected expert readers. The conclusions and interpretations in Russell Sage Foundation publications are those of the authors and not of the Foundation, its Trustees, or its staff. Publication by the Foundation, therefore, does not imply endorsement of the contents of the study.

BOARD OF TRUSTEES
John S. Reed, Chair

Robert McCormick Adams
Earl F. Cheit
Philip E. Converse
Renée Fox

Herma Hill Kay
Carl Kaysen
Patricia King
Gardner Lindzey

Gary MacDougal
James G. March
Madelon Talley
Eric Wanner

Library of Congress Cataloging-in-Publication Data

Moore, Mark Harrison.
  Inspectors-general.

  (Social research perspectives: occasional reports on current topics; 13)
  Bibliography: p.
  1. Finance, Public—United States—Accounting.
  2. Administrative agencies—United States—Auditing.
  3. United States—Executive departments—Auditing.
  I. Gates, Margaret Jane. II. Title. III. Series: Social research perspectives; 13.
  HJ9801.M66 1987   353.0072'32   86-6728
  ISBN 0-87154-605-1

Copyright © 1986 by Russell Sage Foundation. All rights reserved. Printed in the United States of America. No part of this publication may be reproduced, stored in a retrieval system, or transmitted, in any form or by any means, electronic, mechanical, photocopying, recording, or otherwise, without the prior written permission of the publisher.

NOTICE of series title change: *Social Research Perspectives* is a new title for the *Social Science Frontiers* series (volumes 1–9 published 1969–1977). The numbering of *Perspectives* volumes is a continuation of the *Frontiers* numbering.

10 9 8 7 6 5 4 3 2 1

Social Research Perspectives

Occasional Reports on Current Topics from the Russell Sage Foundation

The *Social Research Perspectives* series revives a special format used by the Russell Sage Foundation for nine volumes published from 1969 to 1977 under the series title, *Social Science Frontiers*. The *Frontiers* series established itself as a valuable source of information about significant developments in the social sciences. With the re-named *Perspectives* series, we again provide a timely, flexible, and accessible outlet for the products of ongoing social research—from literature reviews to explorations of emerging issues and new methodologies; from summaries of current policy to agendas for future study and action.

The following *Frontiers* titles are still available:
5 *The Corporate Social Audit*, by Raymond A. Bauer and Dan H. Fenn, Jr. (1972)
7 *Social Forecasting Methodology: Suggestions for Research*, by Daniel P. Harrison (1976)
8 *The Vulnerable Age Phenomenon*, by Michael Inbar (1976)
9 *Work and Family in the United States: A Critical Review and Agenda for Research and Policy*, by Rosabeth Moss Kanter (1977)

Now available in the *Perspectives* series:
10 *Your Time Will Come: The Law of Age Discrimination and Mandatory Retirement*, by Lawrence M. Friedman
11 *Risk Acceptability According to the Social Sciences*, by Mary Douglas
12 *Risk Management and Political Culture: A Comparative Analysis of Science in the Policy Context*, by Sheila Jasanoff

Acknowledgments

The authors would like to acknowledge the assistance of many others in preparing this document. The principal debt is owed to the Russell Sage Foundation, which provided funds to carry out the research and a great deal of encouragement and assistance along the way. We are particularly grateful to Peter de Janosi, Alida Brill, and Priscilla Lewis. In addition, the Alfred P. Sloan Foundation contributed to this effort through its general support to Public Management Research at the Kennedy School. We are particularly grateful to Arthur Singer and Harry Weiner.

In terms of substantive advice and criticism, we benefited a great deal from the comments of Thomas McBride, Thomas Morris, Kurt Muellenberg, and Robert Katzmann. In addition, the community of Inspectors-General were particularly generous with their wisdom and time. In particular, we would like to thank those who attended the special meeting we held in Washington and those who attended the Senior Managers in Government Program at Harvard. We learned an enormous amount from Richard Kusserow, Frank Sato, Charles Dempsey, and John Martin. We would also like to thank Harold Steinberg of the President's Council on Integrity and Efficiency for his willingness to share materials and ideas with us.

We also benefited from the assistance of the Case Program at the Kennedy School of Government. Stephanie Gould, the director, Esther Scott, the chief editor, and Rob Leavitt, a case writer, all contributed enormously to our understanding of the IG function and its impact on government operations.

Finally, we would like to acknowledge the editorial assistance of Gaylen Moore, who wielded her scalpel with grace and precision even when a cleaver would have been more appropriate, and the secretarial assistance of Diana Murray, who has now seen Moore through two books.

While we are grateful for all the assistance we were given, we blame no one but ourselves for any errors that remain.

Contents

1 Inspectors-General and the Demand
  for Accountability   1
2 The Legislative Mandate   9
  The Legislative History   *10*
  Competing Operational Objectives   *16*
  • Detecting Fraud, Waste, and
    Abuse   *17*
  • Prevention Versus Detection of Fraud,
    Waste, and Abuse   *23*
  • Promoting Economy and
    Efficiency   *26*
  • Implications of Different Missions for
    Relations with Program
    Managers   *28*
3 The Presidential Mandate and the Strategies
  of the Inspectors-General   31
  Presidential Mandates for the Offices of
    Inspectors-General   *31*
  The Organizational Strategies of the
    Inspectors-General   *36*

- Organizing and Staffing the Offices 36
- Defining the Work 43
  Reducing Fraud and Abuse Versus Promoting Efficiency 46
  Detection Versus Prevention 47
  Internal Focus Versus External Focus 49
- Relationship with Management 50

4 Evaluating the Impact of the Offices of Inspectors-General 55

  A Compliance Inspection of the Offices of Inspectors-General 58
  A Performance Inspection of the Offices of Inspectors-General 61
  - Enhanced Financial Integrity: The Improved Detection of Fraud and Abuse 61
  - Reduced Costs and the Promotion of Efficiency 64
  - Summary 68
  Relations with Program Management and Political Oversight 70

5 Summary and Conclusions 75

  Conclusions About the Impact of the Offices of Inspectors-General 78
  Recommendations for the Future Development of the Offices of Inspectors-General 81
  - Relationships with Congress and Program Managers 81
  - Terms of Accountability and the Measurement of Performance 83

Appendix A The Concept of Accountability 95

  Different Dimensions of the Accountability Relationship 97
  - The Specificity of the Contract 97
  - Accountability for Outcomes, Outputs, Processes, or Resources 97

- Monitoring Performance   *100*
- The Liability of the Agent   *102*
- The Spirit of the Relationship   *102*

Accountability in the Public Sector   103
- Ambiguity About the Principal and the Purposes   *103*
- Problems in Measurement   *105*
- Third Party Production   *107*
- Innovative Programs   *109*
- Sanctions for Performance   *110*

Summary   112

Appendix B   The Impact of the Offices of Inspectors-General on Program Operations   117

Part I Inspectors-General and the Demand for Accountability

A dominant feature of the American political culture is distrust of government.[1] A corollary is an unquenchable thirst for accountability that cuts across the political spectrum. On the right, conservatives worry that without strict demands for "financial integrity," nothing checks public officials from expanding government programs in pursuit of their own selfish interests, and nothing prevents unscrupulous clients from cheating loose government programs.[2] Similarly, businessmen accustomed to the discipline of the "bottom line" naturally want the same sort of accountability imposed on government.[3] On the left, progressives animated by visions of "good government" hope to scourge corruption and waste with the cleansing power of public oversight and the techniques of "scientific management."[4] Finally, liberals demand assurances that the government will spread its largesse (and impose its duties) fairly and decently rather than arbitrarily and intrusively. Everyone agrees, then, that the evils of corruption, arbitrariness, and inefficiency are inherent in government and that they can be exorcised through mechanisms of accountability.

Although deeply rooted in our political history, the thirst for accountability has also been stimulated by more recent trends. One is the dramatic increase in the size, scope, and complexity of government operations. Over the last two decades, the administrative capacities of government have been strained to the breaking point by an onslaught of legislation mandating broad new regulatory and entitlement programs.[5] Programs such as environmental protection, promotion of safety and health in the workplace, food stamps, medicare, and medicaid would have been politically controversial in any case. But the speed with which they were developed made it almost inevitable that significant administrative weaknesses would appear. And, indeed, scandals involving corrupt officials and unscrupulous clients have been exposed and given wide publicity—thereby confirming the public's generalized suspicions.[6] To a degree, the attacks on program administration are surrogates for political opposition to the programs: instead of attacking the substantive values that these programs are designed to pursue, political opposition focuses on issues of administrative feasibility. But the demands for accountability can be seen as legitimate in their own right as well. Indeed, it is the widespread legitimacy of the values of "tight" administration that makes the *administrative* weaknesses of both defense and welfare programs the focus of attacks even from those whose primary objection to these programs is substantive rather than procedural.

A second important trend influencing the public's demand for accountability has been the faltering domestic economy. "Stagflation" has increased both the actual and the perceived weight of the federal tax burden. To worried federal taxpayers now paying one fifth to one third of their income to the federal government, any sign of "fraud, waste, and abuse" in government is infuriating.[7] It is good politics, then, to rail against the negligent scoundrels in Washington.

A third trend capitalizes on the public's general hostility toward government. Both Presidents Carter and Reagan won elections as outsiders running against Washington's bloated bureaucracy. Their campaign and elections not only revealed but also strengthened the public's determination to root out fraud, waste, and abuse in government.

Given the durability, strength, and salience of these concerns among citizens, it is not surprising that Congress acted to combat fraud, waste, and abuse in government by creating a network of specialized institutions called Offices of Inspectors-General (OIGs).[8] Nor is it surprising that an incoming Republican administration, devoted to reducing the cost of government, would seize on the OIGs as a central instrument of its purposes and make the development of OIGs the principal managerial initiative of the Office of Management and Budget (OMB).[9] The OIGs symbolize a public value that has widespread public appeal: the interest in assuring taxpayers that their hard-earned money, grudgingly given for public purposes, is well spent.

The close connection to a durable public demand guarantees the survival of the OIGs. But the question of survival is less interesting than two more subtle questions: Will the OIGs become prominent and powerful or fade into the background? Will their impact on government credibility and performance be positive or negative?

In considering whether the OIGs will stay as prominent and powerful as they now appear to be, it is well to remember that they are only the most recent institutional response to the public demand for government accountability. In the earliest days of the federal government, bureau chiefs in the executive branch were already accountable to elected political executives, legislative committees, and the courts. More recently, the demand for closer accountability spawned the Bureau of the Budget, the General Accounting Office, and specialized offices of administration and management within executive departments.[10] More recently still, offices of planning and evaluation reaped the rewards and incurred the risks of promising enhanced accountability to a demanding public.[11] While the demand for accountability has been constant, then, its favored institutional vehicle has been far more fickle. This means that the OIGs cannot afford complacency.

Moreover, in gauging the potential impact of the OIGs on government performance and credibility, it is well to remember that the OIGs can do harm as well as good. Of course, the mechanisms through which the OIGs can do good are the most obvious. To the extent that the OIGs strengthen both the incentives and the capabilities of government managers to minimize fraud, waste, and abuse, and thereby decrease the costs of government operations, government efficiency and effectiveness will be enhanced. To the extent that the OIGs can slake the demands for accountability by assuring citizens that a powerful agency is looking after their interests, confidence in government can be restored. All this is obviously beneficial and would justify the investment made in the OIGs.

The mechanisms through which the OIGs could harm government performance and credibility are less obvious, but perhaps no less likely. It is possible, for example, that the motivations and capabilities of government managers to control fraud, waste, and abuse are already strong and that the OIGs add little to the nexus of institutions already devoted to this goal. In this case, the OIGs would *reduce* government efficiency because they would add costs to government operations, but produce no significant improvements. It is also possible that the OIGs could produce changes in government operations that reduced the government's vulnerability to fraud, waste, and abuse, but did so only by harming other valued features of government performance. This could happen, for example, if administrative "controls" proposed by the OIGs to reduce fraud, waste, and abuse made government services slower, less responsive to unusual situations, and more intrusive.[12]

Finally, if the OIGs focused public attention on levels of fraud, waste, and abuse as the only important feature of government performance, and encouraged unreasonably low tolerance of these, the OIGs could weaken both the credibility and the performance of government. To the extent that this weakened credibility discouraged citizens from relying on the government to produce valuable public services such as a strong national defense or decent social "safety nets," the OIGs would harm public sector performance.

Whether the OIGs will remain prominent or fade, and whether their impact will be positive or negative, depends a great deal on strategic choices to be made by those who oversee the development of the OIGs—the Inspectors-General (IGs) themselves and those in the Congress and the White House who take an interest in them. There are, of course, a great many operational questions that are important to the OIGs: for example, how to deploy their resources between audits and investigations; how to distribute limited audit and investigative resources across different programs; whether to rely principally on complaints as a targeting device or to take the initiative in spotting fraud, waste, and abuse on their own; and whether to focus on federal operations or those organizations that receive money from the federal government to accomplish federal purposes.

The more fundamental questions for the Inspectors-General are those that concern the ultimate accountability of the OIGs themselves. They must decide, for example, if they are in business primarily to find previous errors, assign blame, and recapture lost resources, or whether it is more important for them to use information about past errors to design better policies and procedures for the future. Similarly, the IGs must decide whether their important task is to promote fiduciary responsibility (in the sense that managers can account for all the resources entrusted to them and show that they have been used according to existing policies) or to assume a broader responsibility for promoting efficiency (in the sense that, over time, the quantity and quality of government production per unit of cost continues to increase). These are strategic questions because the answers will have an important effect on the support that the OIGs receive from their sponsors in the Congress and the White House (and therefore their survival and prominence), and the OIGs' relations with program managers (and therefore their impact on government operations).

The OIGs, then, are important government institutions. They are the current repository of our hopes for improved public sector accountability and performance. In pursuit of this goal, they can flourish or fade, enhance or erode confidence in government, and facilitate or impede government operations. Moreover, since these results will be determined by important choices made in the next several years, there should be some interest among those who are concerned about government accountability in just how these institutions are developing.

The purpose of this monograph is to provide a preliminary assessment of this important institutional innovation, with the aim of guiding the OIGs toward their most valuable uses and away from potential harms. Our method is both analytical and empirical. The analytical objective is to refine many of the concepts used in discussions of OIG operations: concepts such as "accountability"; "performance"; "efficiency and effectiveness"; "financial integrity"; "fraud, waste, and abuse"; the "prevention of fraud, waste, and abuse"; and the "promotion of efficiency." These concepts are so closely related that they are often treated as a single *gestalt*. But the reality is that these concepts differ in ways that matter to the mission and effectiveness of the OIGs and therefore need to be clarified.

The empirical objective is to trace the development and impact of OIGs throughout the federal government. At the outset, the empirical investigation confronted five problems. (1) The institutions were evolving, not fixed in stone. Thus, our description had to be a blurry picture of a moving target. (2) The OIGs differed from one another. These differences partly reflected different stages of development (some OIGs have existed longer than others), but they also reflected differences in the political and operating environments of the different organizations and the personal judgments of the individuals who became Inspectors-General. (3) The important effects of the OIGs were apt to consist of apparently small changes in procedures or managerial values that would produce large cumulative effects on important, but largely unmeasured, characteristics of government programs. (4) Any observed change in the character of government operations could be explained by factors other than OIG influence. It would be hard to sort out an OIG effect from a general effect of the emergent demand for enhanced accountability and financial integrity. (5) Our resources for investigating the important issues were quite limited.

To solve these problems we relied on the following basic assumptions. First, in describing the OIGs, we decided that it was as important to describe their future trajectory as it was to describe their current operations. The relevant forces operating on the OIGs included their political context (including their legislative mandate and the continuing pressures exerted by oversight agencies in Congress and the White House), their internal dynamics (including tensions between auditors and investigators and substantial differences about how the OIGs should manage their relationships with political overseers and the press, on the one hand, and the program managers, on the other), and the strategic conceptions of the IGs themselves. Indeed, probably the most important clues as to the future of the OIGs would be the philosophies, intentions, and strategies of those who served as IGs, for these would be not only significant causal factors in their own right, but also probably would reveal a great deal about the balance of forces (both external and internal) operating on the OIGs. Thus, an analysis of the legislative history of the statutes establishing OIGs, a review of White House activities with respect to the OIGs, and interviews with the IGs themselves became crucial data for our investigation.

Second, in seeking to characterize the development of the OIGs, it was necessary that we examine a broad enough sample of OIG operations to capture both their central tendencies and their heterogeneity. Since we did not have a great deal of time or money, we had to rely primarily on interviews with the IGs and the reports they submitted. We thought that the way the reports were constructed would give us a clue as to how the IGs thought of themselves even if they failed to give a wholly accurate picture of OIG operations. The interviews with the IGs also produced a great deal of useful information about the differences in capacities of the units they inherited and the problems of the agencies for which they were responsible. While it was not possible to determine precisely the "weighted average" of OIG activities, the interviews and published reports provided a rough sense of what was common and what was different among OIGs.

Third, by far the hardest problem was to determine the short-run and long-run effects of the OIGs on the performance of government programs. We relied on two quite imperfect instruments to measure these effects. The first instrument was to develop cases describing the operations and effects of OIGs in two different departments and four operating programs within them. The departments and programs were chosen because they differed from one another in characteristics that could plausibly affect the magnitude and scale of OIG effects. Thus, we chose the Department of Agriculture because it had had an OIG for a long time and the Department of Labor (DOL) because its experience with OIGs was more recent. We chose the Food Stamp (FS) and Comprehensive Employment and Training Act (CETA) Programs because they were large, administratively complex programs and the Farmer's Home Administration (FmHA) Loan Programs and the Federal Employees Compensation Act (FECA) Program because they were simpler and directly administered by the federal government. We chose FS because it was a welfare program, CETA because it was a treatment-rehabilitation program, and FmHA because it was a loan program.

In addition, we looked at programs that had been the focus of OIG efforts. In this respect, the sampling strategy was deliberately biased: we looked for effects in areas where we could expect to see them. This meant that we could not form any conclusions about the indirect effects of OIGs on program operations, nor about their average impact on programs, but we could get the sharpest possible look at the sorts of effects OIGs produced when they were working hard on a program.

The second instrument we used to measure the impact of OIGs on programs was to hold two meetings attended by both Inspectors-General and program managers who discussed the issue. While the data obtained through this method were less accurate and less precise than the data obtained from the cases, the meetings allowed us to tap into a broader range of departments and programs than could be covered by the cases. In effect, we used these meetings to add breadth across departments and programs to complement the (relative) depth of the cases. As it turned out, these meetings also produced enormously valuable information about an issue that was not originally part of our design—namely, the nature of the engagement between the OIGs and line managers. These conferences caused us to elevate this issue as a separate topic of analysis and to view it as perhaps the most significant factor in determining the long-run impact of the OIGs.

In summary, the kinds of data we had available to investigate the *development* of the OIGs were: (1) an analysis of legislative history, (2) documents describing executive branch initiatives affecting OIGs, (3) interviews with past and present IGs, and (4) annual reports submitted to Congress by the OIGs. The sources of data on their *impact* were: (1) original case studies of two departments and four programs within them, (2) other related case studies, and (3) two conferences of IGs and program managers. In the end, these data seemed quite rickety in terms of their ability to illuminate the nature of the OIG enterprise. But they have the virtue of being at least some data in a world in which little else has been collected.

Part II The Legislative Mandate

On October 12, 1978, following an overwhelmingly favorable vote in Congress, President Carter signed the Inspector-General Act of 1978.[13] This Act mandated the creation of Offices of Inspectors-General in a dozen federal departments: Agriculture, Education, Housing and Urban Development, Interior, Labor, Transportation, Community Services, Environmental Protection, General Services, National Aeronautic and Space, Small Business, and Veterans.[14] The new Offices joined previously established statutory offices in the Departments of Health, Education, and Welfare, and Energy.[15] Later the Act was amended to include an additional three agencies: the Department of Commerce in 1979, the Agency for International Development in 1981, and the Department of Defense in 1982.[16] In addition, a separate statute established an Inspector-General with slightly different functions in the State Department.[17] Thus, eighteen OIGs are now established by statute. Only Justice and Treasury have escaped a statutory requirement, but both agencies have moved administratively to establish organizational units serving the same purposes.[18]

The Act is extremely important in that it provided a statutory basis for already existing Inspectors-General and dramatically expanded their use throughout the federal government. But like most other statutes, the Act was based on prior experience with broadly comparable institutions. Moreover, it left room for the newly established Offices to develop in many different directions. Our task in this chapter is to develop a sense of both the current trajectory and future possibilities of the OIGs. This requires an understanding of the legislative mandate and continuing congressional concerns that breathe life into the existing OIGs and an idea of the varied operational paths the Inspectors-General might have taken in response to their mandate. The next chapter will examine the implementation of the Inspector-General Act as it has been influenced by presidential initiatives and interests and the IGs' own strategies.

The Legislative History

Leadership for the creation of statutory OIGs throughout the 1970s came from the Government Operations Committee of the House of Representatives, and particularly from the chairman of the committee, Representative Jack Brooks (D, Texas), the committee counsel, James Naughton, and the chairman of the Sub-Committee on Intergovernmental Relations and Human Resources, L. H. Fountain (D, North Carolina).[19] The legislation they envisioned was ambitious: it proposed a substantial and detailed reorganization of investigative and audit capabilities in a dozen federal departments into centralized Offices of Inspectors-General; it gave these Offices complete autonomy and substantial powers in conducting investigations; and perhaps most important, it gave the Inspector-General himself some protection against arbitrary firing by political executives. It also required the IGs to report to Congress as well as directly to the secretary of the relevant department.[20] In short, the legislation created a powerful instrument to root out fraud, waste, and abuse in government and make it an instrument of Congress as well as the executive branch. Indeed, many in the executive branch regarded the OIGs as congressional "moles" within their agencies, and the Department of Justice believed that the congressional intrusion into executive branch operations was so substantial that it violated the Separation of Powers doctrine.[21]

Despite the scope of the legislation and the determined opposition of the executive branch, the House Committee on Government Operations had several crucial resources that enhanced prospects for passage. One was the existence of favorable operating experience with institutions similar to those being proposed in the legislation. In 1962, in response to the Billie Sol Estes scandal, Secretary of Agriculture Orville Freeman consolidated the audit and investigative resources of ten major programs into a single Office of the Inspector-General for the purpose of providing him with "an independent and objective review and appraisal" of his operations.[22] (Estes had been revealed to have parlayed fraudulent warehouse receipts, mortgages, and financial statements into a fortune from the Department of Agriculture despite the fact that his activities were suspected by three different audit units within the department.) In 1968 the General Accounting Office (GAO) reported favorably on the operations of this unit.[23] Indeed, the GAO's only criticism was that the Office had not gone far enough in exercising control over audit and investigative activities in the Department of Agriculture (USDA) and that it should direct itself not so much to the discovery of individual instances of scandal, but to "broader based reviews" of program operations.[24] In 1972 the Department of Housing and Urban Development (HUD) followed USDA's lead and established its own Office of Inspector-General in response to the urging of Lester Condon, the first Inspector-General at USDA, who had gone to HUD as an Assistant Secretary in 1969.[25]

Congressional interest in OIGs then faded, and the existing OIGs began to lose ground in their agencies until 1974 when congressional interest was aroused by press reports indicating widespread cheating in two major programs within the Department of Health, Education, and Welfare (HEW)—medicare and student loans. The House Committee on Government Operations began an investigation into HEW's resources and procedures for combating fraud and abuse, and Representative Benjamin Rosenthal (D, New York) introduced a bill to establish an Office of Inspector-General in HEW.[26] In this bill, the IG was basically a law enforcement officer who was appointed for a nonrenewable term of ten years. He was granted significant powers to subpoena records and witnesses. His job was to discover significant instances of fraud and abuse within HEW's massive programs.[27] The Senate, too, was investigating fraud in HEW under the leadership of Senator Frank E. Moss (D, Utah) and his Sub-

Committee of the Special Committee on Aging.[28] Posing as patients in clinics that were described as "Medicaid Mills," the staff of this subcommittee had discovered instances of poor and unnecessary treatment, fraudulent billings, and kickbacks.[29] These investigations led to renewed legislative interest in IGs and culminated in the passage of the HEW Inspector-General Act in 1976.[30]

An important new feature of the debate surrounding the HEW bill was the issue of the OIG's "independence." Much of the earlier debate had focused on the organization, powers, procedures, and targets of OIG activity. Everyone seemed to agree that the Office should be powerful and visible, and therefore it should report to the highest levels of the departments. Now, for the first time however, the Congress began thinking that the OIG should be made independent even of the Secretary, lest the Secretary be tempted to quash investigations or ignore OIG recommendations. To a degree, "independence" could be assured by the professional qualifications and integrity of those who became IGs and by providing them with protection against firing. But, in the tradition of political thought in the United States, independence could truly be assured only if the IGs were made accountable to someone other than the Secretary—for example, the Congress. Predictably, this was more appealing to Congress than it was to the executive branch. Executive branch witnesses reserved their sharpest criticisms for this feature of the proposed act.[31] Congress, nonetheless, found the arguments compelling, and mandatory reporting to Congress was included in the legislation that ultimately passed.[32]

By 1978, then, Congress had fairly wide experience with the issues surrounding the creation of OIGs and some evidence to indicate that OIGs could be successful in uncovering, and therefore presumably controlling, fraud and abuse in government. That alone, however, would probably not have been sufficient to pass the 1978 legislation. What Congress had come to believe by 1978 that it had not previously accepted was that government programs were rotten with massive fraud, waste, and abuse and that neither the political executives nor the career civil servants who managed the programs could be relied on to root it out.

This widespread perception was based on analyses of government operations and documented instances of personal corruption at high policy levels of the government, as well as at operating levels.[33] There was no necessary logical connection between the two different problems, of course. There could be substantial fraud, waste, and abuse in programs even if high-level officials were squeaky clean. And there could be substantial integrity in the bulk of program operations even if individual high-level officials were abusing their offices for private gain. Nonetheless, these issues became fused in the public mind, and they eventually determined the central features of the Inspector-General Act of 1978: namely, the determination to make the Offices large and powerful; to focus the OIGs' attention on the elimination of fraud, waste, and abuse; and to make OIGs independent of executive branch political executives who could not be trusted to discover and control abuses in their operating programs. In effect, Congress cast itself in the role of cleaning up government—an idea that had always been important to Committees on Government Operations, but by 1978 had also become important to the entire Congress. It is not surprising that the bill passed and that President Carter signed it despite constitutional concerns about the usurpation of executive branch powers by Congress. Indeed, the power of the fraud issue was evident in the votes cast in Congress for its passage—388 to 6 in the House and by voice vote in the Senate.[34]

The implicit theory of the Inspector-General Act of 1978 is that fraud, waste, and abuse can be most effectively controlled by changing the way that information about these aspects of government operations is developed and reported within each agency, and between branches of government. Somewhat more specifically, the Act is designed to accomplish two broad purposes: to increase the overall scale and effectiveness of audit and investigative activities among the twelve federal departments included within the act and to make these activities visible by assuring that the information developed in audits and investigations reaches the highest levels of departments, the Congress, and the American public rather than being stifled at lower levels of the bureaucracy.

The Act seeks to increase the overall scale and effectiveness of audit and investigation not so much by granting additional resources for this purpose, but by reorganizing the existing resources. One aspect of this reorganization is the centralization of all audit and investigative activities within a single office reporting directly to the secretary of the relevant department. Conceivably this reorganization could result in additional resources being provided to these tasks since the concentration and elevation of audit and investigative function would give to OIGs an advantage in inevitable departmental budget fights.[35] But even if no additional resources are forthcoming, the centralization is expected to increase the overall effectiveness of audit and investigation by enhancing the morale of auditors and investigators, and by allowing them to share information and develop their professional skills to the maximum degree. In effect, they will enjoy professional status and camaraderie that are missing in a world in which the auditors and investigators are scattered among operating programs and, most important, subordinated to lower-level program managers.

A second aspect of the reorganization is to place auditors and investigators in the same office. Their separate professional identities are protected by legislative provisions requiring separate Assistant Inspectors-General (AIGs) for Investigation and for Audit.[36] But in combining the two functions within a single office, there seems to be an expectation that the overall effect on corruption will be greater than the sum of the parts.

The two different approaches offer distinct, but complementary, methods for locating instances of fraud, waste, and abuse. Investigators generally initiate cases in response to complaints. They naturally think in terms of hot lines, rewards for information, and the development of potential informants throughout the various departments. Auditors, on the other hand, tend to be proactive rather than reactive—to work on routine schedules that eventually bring them into contact with all the programs within a given department. This breadth means that auditors might find abuse even in situations in which no witness comes forward to point it out. To a degree, one can compare investigators to police detectives who respond to alarms by others and auditors to police patrolmen who systematically patrol the streets looking for violations on their own. Together, then, the investigators and auditors would have the best chance of locating instances of abuse. In addition, there might well be opportunities for operational coordination. Auditors might turn up leads for investigators. Investigators might hear complaints that could reasonably trigger audits.

Another complementary feature of investigation and audit is that the two together provide a much more varied response to instances of fraud than either alone. Investigators tend naturally to think in terms of criminal investigations focused on guilty individuals. Their aim is to produce criminal prosecutions of individuals. Auditors tend to think in terms of program reviews focused on administrative arrangements as well as individual conduct. Their aim is administrative sanctions against negligent managers or new administrative procedures designed to prevent future problems. In diagnosing the conditions that give rise to fraud, waste, and abuse, and in fashioning responses to specific instances, then, the combination of the two approaches offers more options for managing the problem justly and effectively.

In sum, Congress chose the usual governmental response to an emerging political demand for some new purpose or value to be expressed in the operations of government—the creation of a separate, strengthened administrative unit whose primary goal is to advance the purpose or value that justified its creation. Like the Departments of Energy and Education, and the Office of Drug Abuse Prevention, the Inspectors-General were established as an institutional salient for advancing a particular social value. In the case of the OIGs, that value is the minimization of fraud, waste, and abuse in government.

Congress went further than the creation of a powerful organization to advance its interests. It also ensured the continued vitality of the organization and its mission by enhancing the visibility and independence of the OIGs, thereby giving the offices a continuing chance to attract political support from Congress and political executives in the executive branch. The provisions that accomplished this aim follow:

1. IGs are appointed by the President regardless of political affiliation, and removed by the President only after giving reasons to Congress.[37]
2. IGs report directly to the Secretary.[38]
3. IGs have direct and full authority to initiate, carry out, or complete audits and investigations without interference from the President, cabinet secretaries, or program managers.[39]
4. IGs have a general obligation to keep the Secretary and the Congress informed of problems and recommended actions.[40]
5. IGs have more specific obligations to report serious problems to the Secretary who must in turn provide the reports to Congress within seven days, and to provide semiannual

reports to Congress of problems, corrective actions proposed and implemented, criminal referrals, and provide other reports done for the Secretary as part of routine operations.[41]

6. IGs have a general obligation to make audit reports available to the general public.[42]

Given the amount of interest and attention that would be focused on any indication of fraud, waste, and abuse in government, the OIGs' broad responsibilities to report publicly not only on the magnitude of problems but also on the progress of proposed corrective actions would make the OIGs very influential in shaping the character of government operations.

Competing Operational Objectives

While there was widespread enthusiasm for the general goals of the OIGs, there was greater uncertainty about the relative importance of more specific operational objectives. If we examine the legislative history closely, we find that most of the incidents that spurred legislative indignation involved outright fraud rather than the more subtle instances of waste or abuse.[43] Consequently, we might reasonably imagine that the OIGs' central mission is to ferret out fraud and punish the offenders. But the ultimate language of the statute is much broader than this. It establishes a responsibility for attacking something called waste and abuse as well as fraud. And it goes beyond the *detection* of fraud, waste, and abuse to charge the OIGs with *prevention* as well. Perhaps most surprising, the legislation gives the OIGs the responsibility for *promoting economy and effectiveness,* as well as controlling fraud, waste, and abuse.[44]

From the legislative perspective, this broad mandate is entirely sensible. After all, the instances of outright fraud can be seen as the mere tip of an iceberg, indicating volumes of waste and abuse just beneath the surface of government operations. Similarly, while there is some virtue in detecting current problems and disciplining those who are guilty or careless, there must be even greater virtue in figuring out how to prevent future instances of abuse. Finally, since reductions in fraud, waste, and abuse should reduce the costs of government operations and leave output unaffected, more effective control over government corruption seems consistent with the overarching goal of promoting economy and effectiveness. So, the mandate hangs together as a general congressional exhortation to government to clean up its act.

From an analytic and operational perspective, however, the concepts of fraud, waste, and abuse are quite different; the idea of detecting current abuse is quite different from preventing future problems; and the idea of promoting economy and effectiveness is quite different from the idea of controlling fraud, waste, and abuse. The task of this section of the monograph is to develop the important distinctions among these concepts which seem to fit so naturally together.

DETECTING FRAUD, WASTE, AND ABUSE

Probably the most often repeated phrase in the legislative history of the Inspector-General Act is the phrase "fraud, waste, and abuse." Although the phrase is now common enough to treat as a single concept, it actually includes several distinct ideas. The basic concept that ties the words together (and makes the phrase politically potent) is that some productive value, potentially available to the government, is being lost: that somehow the public is not getting what it intended to buy, or as much of what it intended to buy. What distinguishes the separate ideas of fraud, waste, and abuse are distinctions that originate in the culpability of those who inflict the loss on the government and the objectivity with which a certain loss can be established.

Fraud is the clearest concept. It defines situations in which some potential claimant against the government (for example, a contractor or client) willfully misrepresents some fact that entitles him to something of value from the government (for example, a payment for services to the contractor or the delivery of a benefit to clients), and the government provides the payment or service even though it is undeserved (for example, the contractors have done no work for the government or the client is ineligible for the government benefit). For example, a physician might bill for services he never provided, a food stamp recipient might lie about the size of his family, or a government employee might report continuing disability in order to continue receiving his full disability payments despite the fact that he has become partially employed. In such cases, the government pays out tax dollars even though nothing of value—nothing that the government wished to provide or create—is produced in the transaction. An important additional aspect of fraud is that the person who receives the payment actively deceives the government. He knows what he is doing and means to do it. This is what makes fraud a criminal act punishable by criminal statutes rather than a careless act punishable by administrative action or loss of professional reputation.

The concepts of waste and abuse are inherently more ambiguous. Like fraud, they suggest that something of potential value to the government is being lost—that funds are being paid out and services provided but without any benefit to the government or the public. One difference is that the culpability of the person responsible for the loss seems less. In the case of abuse, the culprit may be badly motivated, but not clearly in violation of any laws. The official may have taken advantage of some loophole in the structure of rules guiding expenditures within a program to benefit himself or others in a way that differs from the common understanding of what the rules intend. For example, in one of our cases, FmHA officials provided a low-interest loan under its Emergency Loan Program to a farm that had suffered damage from drought, but also happened to be owned by a wealthy corporation that was only incidentally in the business of farming.[45] Neither the corporation nor the officials lied about anything, nor did they violate any rules, but it seemed to many that FmHA officials were tempted to use government resources in ways that were not intended by Congress. Even worse, it seemed that they made the deal snickering all the while.

In the case of waste, the culpability seems even less: it suggests negligence or incompetence rather than sharp-dealing within the rules. Officials aren't perceived to be advancing their own interests or those of friends. They are just being less careful than they should be with the government's money. For example, a major portion of the "waste" identified by the OIG in HEW in the late 1970s involved government payments for "excessive hospital capacity," "unnecessary surgery," and "excessive hospital stays."[46] On a much smaller scale, the "waste" identified in FmHA's Emergency Loan Program involved the failure to "graduate" clients of the program to ordinary commercial loans when it became feasible;[47] and "waste" in the FECA programs involved insufficient use of rehabilitative services to return disabled federal employees to gainful employment.[48]

What makes waste and abuse more ambiguous than fraud is

not only the difference in the apparent culpability of the person responsible for the lost productive value, but also the objectivity with which the loss can be established. The problem is not in establishing that a government expenditure took place, which generally can be quickly established, but in determining whether something of value sufficient to justify the expenditure resulted from that expenditure. In the case of fraud, we know the answer to that question is no. In the case of waste and abuse, the society has the OIG's assertion that an expenditure was abusive or wasteful. But by what criterion is the society to judge that assertion?

One answer is that the society should judge whether something of sufficient value has been produced on the basis of a more or less common understanding of the government's intended purposes within a given program. For example, the purpose of the FmHA Emergency Loan Program is to help poor farmers, not wealthy corporations; and the goal of medicaid is to provide the minimum amount of required care rather than keep hospitals filled and their overhead covered. It is against this common understanding that a given expenditure can be deemed abusive or wasteful.

A second answer relies on the rules that exist to govern a program. Some rules are substantive and set out specific purposes for which expenditures may be made. Others are procedural and describe the steps that must be taken before a given expenditure is made. Obviously, if these rules are specific, and if it can be shown that a given expenditure violates the rules, then we can establish that an incidence of waste or abuse has occurred even if there is no fraud.

The difference between these two criteria is quite obvious. In relying on the first criterion, an IG charging that an expenditure is wasteful or abusive would be taking a lot of responsibility on himself. He would be claiming that he knows what Congress intends or, even more provocatively, that he knows the real value of a given expenditure even without congressional guidance, and those who made the expenditure do not. In relying on the second criterion, he would be on much firmer ground. In describing an expenditure as wasteful or abusive, he could refer to a relatively clear rule that was violated, and this would be his proof, regardless of the actual effect of the expenditure and the wishes of Congress.

It is for this reason that the existence of relatively precise rules setting out proper purposes for expenditures and procedures for authorizing expenditures are fundamental to an IG's ability to detect waste and abuse. If there are no rules, or the rules are ambiguous, the IG's assertion that given expenditures are abusive or wasteful becomes a subjective judgment. In effect, he pits his judgment about what is valuable, and how some valuable purpose might be most effectively pursued, against the judgments of others—particularly the program managers who authorized the expenditure that is now deemed to be wasteful or abusive.

This is an extremely difficult position for the IGs. The reason is that the credibility of the IGs lies in their being "objective" and "independent" in their judgments. Of course, it is possible to be relatively objective in making the judgment that a given expenditure violated a relatively specific rule. Lacking the rule, the IGs are necessarily thrown back on general arguments about the value of the expenditure. These arguments inevitably seem "subjective" or "political" because they concern values rather than facts. One person's "waste" is another person's "quality service."

Moreover, in carrying on the discussions about the value of an expenditure in the absence of a preannounced rule, the IGs are dominated by others. In determining the value of given programs, they must yield to the judgments of "policy-makers" such as Congress, the President, and presidential appointees because that is the task for which they are elected, appointed, and reviewed. In determining the best ways to achieve given purposes, IGs must yield to program managers—both appointed and career—for they are far more knowledgeable in the substantive areas they manage than the IGs can ever be. To avoid this difficulty, then, the IGs must rely on rules to define "proper" expenditures. That is the only way that they can retain their independence and objectivity in dealing with the essentially normative question of whether an expenditure is wasteful or abusive, and the substantive complexity of the many programs they must investigate or audit.

From the vantage point of policy-makers and managers, however, the IGs' push for preannounced rules creates difficulties. To the extent that managers need discretion to deal with unexpected or unusual cases, or to experiment with different ways of handling familiar cases, the IGs' desire to establish comprehensive rules will frustrate these ambitions. Some potential value in the operation will be sacrificed in the interest of assuring the objectivity with which waste and abuse can be defined. Moreover, managers will feel that they are in a better position to judge the overall value of a program than the IGs whose interests in minimizing fraud, waste, and abuse seem narrower than the managers' interests in producing high quality programs at low cost. Thus, managers might reasonably resist the drive to narrow discretion, not simply to defend their prerogatives and power, but also to preserve some flexibility and adaptability to maximize the value of the programs.

The most difficult situations are not those in which the rules are nonexistent, and not those in which the OIGs and policymakers are negotiating more specific rules to guide expenditures, but in situations in which the OIGs disagree with the policymakers about the value of a governmental enterprise but find it convenient to attack a program on its failure to comply with rules rather than on substantive grounds. A revealing example of this sort of problem occurred within FmHA's Business and Industrial Loan Program.[49] In the fall of 1980, President Carter and the Congress had committed the government to experiments with "gasohol production" as part of the nation's efforts to increase its energy independence. Legislation was passed launching this new program, which would not take effect until several months later. FmHA was to assume part of the responsibility for the new program. At the time, however, FmHA had funds available in an older program—its Business and Industrial Loan Program. Moreover, some proposals for "gasohol" projects were then pending with this program. Instead of waiting for the new program, FmHA officials went ahead and made a series of substantial loans to support "gasohol" projects under the existing Business and Industrial Loan Program. The loans were immediately investigated by OIG, which charged that the officials who initiated this move were involved in "abuses" because in their haste to make the loans they cut corners in the required procedures. Eventually the loans were "de-obligated" and the applications sent back for additional review. The review produced some changes in the applications, but most, once again, were approved.

This is a good example of the OIG operating on a definition of waste or abuse that depends on procedural rules for its definition. What is significant, however, is that at least part of the motivation for OIG disapproval of these loans was not the officials' failure to follow required procedures, but a view among the auditors that the "gasohol" enterprise was a foolish waste of government resources. As one of the auditors from OIG remarked: "In my opinion, they shouldn't have been making these loans to begin with. . . . [Alcohol fuels] didn't seem like . . . a long-term, feasible solution to anything; it was just a short-term, patch-it-up kind of solution. And, in that sense, *we really did what we set out to do*." [Emphasis added.][50] To the extent that government support to gasohol was without value to the country, the auditors might well congratulate themselves for eliminating this wasteful program. But one can reasonably ask whether the auditors were the best ones to make a policy judgment about the value of this program. Perhaps the judgments of the President, the Congress, and the program managers about the value and feasibility of the program should have greater weight.

The conjunction of fraud, waste, and abuse may serve the OIGs well in terms of sustaining a legislative mandate—with indignation about fraud providing the primary political impetus and operations to control waste and abuse providing the most interesting and compelling work of the organization. But the conjunction also creates significant operating problems. Part of the problem comes from a tension between the desire to attack all of these sources of lost public value, on the one hand, and the desire to remain objective, on the other. As we have seen, it is relatively easy to be objective about fraud. It is harder to be objective about waste and abuse because it requires some specific definition of the appropriate uses of government resources against which to measure current practices. This is what provides the standard against which the OIG may make an objective determination. But bringing all or most of the government's operations under relatively clear operational guidance has the effect of strangling programs in red tape, and freezing the operating technology of the programs, to say nothing of the costs of developing, updating, and revising the myriad of regulations.[51]

A second difficulty in combining fraud, waste, and abuse in a single mandate has to do with maintaining an appropriate balance between investigations and audits not only in terms of the volume of activity carried out by the two units, but also in terms of the overall style of the organization and its relationship to line managers. If fraud were the most important objective of the OIGs, for example, they would probably maximize their performance by organizing themselves to resemble a police department. They would rely on auditors to play the role of patrolling police on the lookout for instances of fraud. They would supplement the auditors' patrols with hot lines or develop internal informants to alert them to instances of fraud. The heaviest investment would be made in investigators who would play the role of detective in developing evidence against those who were defrauding the government. The relationship with the rest of the organization would be distant and suspicious, even adversarial.

If, on the other hand, the principal targets of the OIGs were abuse and waste rather than fraud, then their operations might more properly be dominated by the activities and styles of auditors, for it is they who are primarily interested in these matters. Moreover, auditors understand that the most appropriate relationship for them to have with the program managers is less sharply adversarial. They must negotiate with managers over their conclusions about which expenditures are inappropriate. Often, program managers can give good reasons why resources are used in a particular way. That is why auditors identify questionable expenditures as "audit exceptions" rather than clearly inappropriate, and why audit exceptions are usually negotiated downward.[52] In these negotiations with program managers, the auditor's suspicion that the manager might be cheating is distinctly disadvantageous.

Therefore, in allocating resources between investigation and audit, and in developing a style and a relationship with the rest of the organization, the OIGs must choose between focusing on fraud and abuse, on the one hand (in which investigations, standards, and sternness would be dominant), and focusing on abuse and waste, on the other (in which audits, negotiations over standards, and cooperation would be dominant). Moreover, they must make this choice in a world in which no one is quite sure which is the larger problem, whether measured in terms of actual productive value lost or in terms of perceived public scandal.

PREVENTION VERSUS DETECTION OF FRAUD, WASTE, AND ABUSE

The nature of the IG mission becomes even more complicated if we include in it the job of preventing future fraud, waste, and abuse, as well as detecting current violations. The argument in favor of prevention is very clear. Everyone can see the futility of attacking individual instances of fraud, waste, or abuse.[53] And everyone would much prefer wholesale solutions. The problem arises when we consider how best to accomplish that goal.

To some degree, there is a deterrent effect derived from improved current efforts to detect instances of fraud, waste, and abuse. In this sense, improved current detection has a preventative effect. In addition, however, those who established the OIGs hoped that some "controls" could be created that would make it harder for individual clients, contractors, or employees to engage in fraud, waste, or abuse.[54] An analogy in the criminal justice area would be the distinction between the deterrent effects of patrol and investigation, on the one hand, and "target hardening" such as streetlights, locks, and alarm systems, on the other.

Typically, the controls include some combination of clearly defined procedures for spending resources, creating records (called "audit trails") that can be examined by outsiders to see who authorized an expenditure, and establishing multiple sign-offs for the utilization of specific resources.[55] In some instances, controls may also include special efforts to guard against forged documents or signatures. Just as locks and alarms function as obstacles to street crime, these controls create obstacles to defrauding the government by making the offenses more visible to more people over a longer period of time than they would be without the controls. Of course, these controls work best in a situation in which auditors and investigators are prepared to notice and respond to the alarms given off by the control systems, for these systems are not self-enforcing. But it is probably true that the overall effectiveness of any given number of auditors and investigators is increased by the existence of administrative controls, just as the effectiveness of a municipal police department might be increased by the creation of an elaborate network of locks and alarms or surveillance cameras, and the effectiveness of the Border Patrol might be increased by the creation of remote sensing devices.

Increased effectiveness in preventing fraud, waste, and abuse with administrative controls comes at a price, of course. Each new element of control adds an administrative step. Each step consumes the time, and therefore money, of the official who must take that step and the supervisor or auditor who must review whether the step was taken. Each step and each checkpoint may reduce the initiative and sense of responsibility of individual government workers. And each step will slow down the speed with which a government service may be provided or an obligation imposed. For example, in the FmHA Emergency Loan Program the decision to require a farmer who has suffered a natural disaster to provide additional documentation of his efforts to obtain credit from commercial sources, or to improve the government's estimate of the magnitude of his loss by on-site examinations and the provision of additional financial records, may enhance the precision of the government's response to his situation, but at the expense of slowing down the process and increasing the cost per case handled.[56] Such prices may be worth paying if a new administrative control succeeds in substantially reducing the amount of fraud, waste, and abuse. But the point is that a price must be paid for this benefit, and it is at least theoretically possible that the price could be greater than the benefit.

Fraud, waste, and abuse could also be prevented by redesigning a program to make it less vulnerable. Of course, a program could be eliminated entirely. If fraud, waste, and abuse were so extensive in some programs that they were utterly ineffective, this might be the appropriate response.[57] A more typical situation, however, is one in which a government program has some embarrassing loopholes or some administrative requirements that are simply impossible to honor. For example, the FmHA Emergency Loan Program established no limits on the size of the company that could apply for loans or the amount of aid that could be offered.[58] The CETA Program required annual audits of prime sponsors, but provided insufficient audit resources to achieve this purpose. Thus, it sometimes may be possible to reduce fraud, waste, and abuse as well as reduce administrative costs by *simplifying* eligibility standards rather than complicating them: for example, by examining a smaller number of characteristics and tolerating less verification.[59] Similarly, if it were decided that speed in making government decisions is an unimportant performance characteristic, fraud, waste, and abuse could be reduced by slowing down government operations—for example, by eliminating the special emergency provisions in the Food Stamp Program.[60] Or if policy-makers simply narrowed the scope of a program or eliminated areas in which fraud, waste, and abuse were particularly prominent, they would succeed in preventing them, for example, by eliminating the CETA Public Sector Employment Program or the FmHA Business and Industrial Loan Program.[61]

All of these actions, however, have a price. Here the price registers not as an increase in administrative costs, but instead as a reduction in either the quantity or the quality of government services rendered. If eligibility standards are simplified, there may be less fraud, waste, and abuse (measured in terms of the new eligibility standards); but precisely because the new standards are crude, something may be lost in terms of the precision with which services are provided or obligations enforced. Similarly, if government services are slowed down to allow more time for checking and review, administrative costs will rise, and one important aspect of government service—namely, the speed with which the aid can be provided—will deteriorate. And if all or part of a program is eliminated, not only is fraud, waste, and abuse in the program eliminated, but also whatever benefits are associated with the program. The reductions in the quantity or quality of government services could be large or small, highly valued or negligible in importance. The point is that many efforts to prevent corruption by changing the substantive character of the program will have a price, just as installing administrative controls do. Policy-makers must decide whether the improved prevention of fraud, waste, and abuse is worth the reduction in the quantity and quality of the government services.

PROMOTING ECONOMY AND EFFICIENCY

The difficulty in making a judgment about the value of proposed administrative "controls" indicates why the objective of "promoting economy and efficiency" is by far the most problematic objective included within the OIGs' broad mandate, and the most fundamental. This goal often seems identical with the objective of "attacking fraud, waste, and abuse" since it seems axiomatic that if unproductive uses of resources can be eliminated, efficiency will increase. What separates the concept of "minimizing fraud, waste, and abuse" from the concept of "promoting efficiency," however, is the observation that prices must be paid for controlling abuses. As we have seen, this price is paid in terms of increased administrative costs associated with paying people to audit and investigate; increasingly elaborate procedures which consume resources, blunt operational initiative and responsibility, and freeze operating technologies; or the reduced value of government output in either quantity or quality of the services provided. Thus, it is possible to reduce fraud, waste, and abuse and at the same time *reduce* efficiency! This occurs when the prices paid for controlling corruption are greater than the value of the fraud, waste, and abuse that is prevented.

The difficulty in understanding the concept of promoting efficiency is identical to the difficulty in understanding the problem of "abuse" and "waste": it requires one to think about the *value* of government outputs. Efficiency is concerned not with reducing total costs, but with improving the *relationship* between costs and the value of the output that resulted from incurring the costs. All businessmen know that they must spend money in order to make money. They must spend on plant and equipment, on materials, and on wages in order to make products that can be sold to produce revenues. Similarly, the government must spend money on space, on benefits, and on salaries in order to achieve its purposes—whether those purposes are to build missiles to defend the country, to give loans to farmers who have suffered natural disasters, or to provide income to those who through no fault of their own have become disabled or unemployed.

The important question about efficiency, then, is not simply how much the government spends, *but how much social value it creates through its expenditures*. And that, of course, depends on a *political* judgment about how much the various enterprises of government are worth, relative to the costs measured in terms of dollars spent and authority imposed. Since this is always a contested matter, the whole concept of efficiency remains badly defined. It is something that program managers wrestle with every day as they try to express the proper balance of values in their operations. They must face the consequences of close political scrutiny if they fail to strike the right balance. Moreover, it is particularly difficult for managers to do this confidently if they are operating in a world in which the proper balance of values is contested and technologies for accomplishing their purposes are changing. Inspectors-General can enter into this ambiguous world and try to aid program managers in making this judgment, but the price is that they leave some of their precious objectivity behind; along with their objectivity goes some of their power. IGs can offer advice on promoting efficiency, but at this stage they become colleagues and advisers to program managers rather than overseers or evaluators.

IMPLICATIONS OF DIFFERENT MISSIONS FOR RELATIONS WITH PROGRAM MANAGERS

Table 1 seeks to distinguish the different potential operating missions of the OIGs and show their relationship to one another and to other mechanisms designed to enhance accountability or increase the efficiency and effectiveness of government. The table is constructed by identifying the possible targets of OIG efforts. The horizontal dimension distinguishes between controlling costs, on the one hand, and improving the relationship between cost and output, on the other. Moreover, within the category of controlling cost, it distinguishes between controlling fraud, controlling abuse, and controlling waste. The vertical dimension distinguishes between efforts that are essentially "backward-looking" and devoted to reclaiming lost resources or determining what happened and efforts that are "forward-looking" and aimed at solving problems in the future. In general, the upper left-hand side of the table defines the most traditional audit and investigative function. Movements either down or to the right of the table draw the OIGs into the realm of more speculative, less "objective" judgments. Moving down the table, they must make *predictions* about how measures they propose will affect losses to fraud, waste, and abuse and total costs. Moving to the right in the table, they must make assessments of the *value* of particular government products. Moving down and to the right involves them in

Table 1 The Range of Possible Operating Missions for OIGs

	Controlling Costs			Managing Relationship Between Cost and Output
	Controlling Fraud	Controlling Abuse	Controlling Waste	Promoting Efficiency and Effectiveness
Backward-Looking Detection	Criminal investigation		Audit	Program evaluation
Forward-Looking Prevention		Design of internal controls		Policy analysis, and
Promotion of Efficiency and Economy		Incentives and advice for managers		Program design and experimentation

28

policy design. As the OIGs move down the table, they find themselves invading the traditional domain of Offices of Administration and Management, the GAO, OMB, and so on. As they move across, they find themselves invading the province of Offices of Planning and Evaluation.

Wherever they go, they wind up in an important relationship with the program managers whose operations they scrutinize, though the relationship differs depending on which mission they emphasize. The OIGs' narrowest mission is fraud detection and prosecution—the traditional tasks of internal investigative units. This mission often pits the manager against the OIGs since the appearance of fraud in a program may imply neglect on the part of the manager. Indeed, the conflict may be particularly sharp if someone other than the manager alerts the OIG to the problem, or if the manager himself is under suspicion. Somewhat broader is the mission of detecting waste and abuse—the traditional tasks of inspection and audit. In one way this task is less threatening to managers because the accusation is less serious. On the other hand, the matters under scrutiny in these areas are often broader and more clearly within the powers of the managers to control than they are in fraud, and therefore conceivably a more powerful indictment of them as managers. In the end, though, both fraud investigations and audits must be accepted by managers as a condition of managerial life—part of the apparatus that holds them accountable in exchange for their higher pay and status.

Where real trouble among the IGs, managers, and policymakers may begin is when the mission of the IGs widens to include the development of management systems that are designed to prevent fraud, waste, and abuse. At this stage, the IGs are no longer simply observing program operations to detect isolated problems. Instead, they are proposing changes in procedures that will alter the character of the product or service being delivered, and therefore the value of the program. It is at this stage that the OIGs' interests in minimizing corruption collides with the managers' broader interests in maximizing the difference between the cost of a program and the value of its products and services. In this collision, there is a risk that the OIGs' objectives may become too dominant—that the goal of minimizing fraud, waste, and abuse will take precedence over the broader goal of efficiency for the reason that this goal is politically popular and it seems relatively concrete and well defined compared with the much vaguer idea of maximizing the social value created by a given level of expenditure.

There is, however, a great deal of potential for a useful and creative compromise among IGs, policy-makers, and managers in this encounter. Program managers, who have been preoccupied with the quantity and quality of service provided and have been ignoring costs in general, or the special kinds of costs associated with fraud and abuse that erode the overall credibility of the program, may learn that they can install procedures that cost them little in terms of administrative costs or the value of their output, but dramatically reduce fraud and abuse. IGs who have been examining fraud and abuse may be able to develop ideas that could help managers run their programs more successfully and lend their political weight to the tasks of persuading political overseers in the Congress and executive branch that the changes would be valuable. This is a world in which the IGs and program managers both commit themselves to the difficult task of promoting efficiency.

This situation can easily deteriorate, however. The program managers may assume that the IGs have little to offer in promoting efficiency and therefore refuse to take their advice. The IGs may think that minimizing fraud and abuse is the only important goal of the program, that they alone know best how to achieve this objective, and that all procedures should be bent to this task without worrying about the quantity and quality of services provided. Rather than negotiate with the managers, then, the IGs may leak their reports to Congress or the news media to increase the pressure on program managers to adopt their recommendations.[62] Avoiding this situation requires not only great restraint, skill, and commitment to the cause of government efficiency by both sides, but also restraint and artful guidance from those above the IGs and program managers such as congressional oversight committees and cabinet secretaries. It also requires a political context that facilitates negotiation and compromise. That, in turn, depends a great deal on how Congress and the President choose to use the OIGs.

Part III The Presidential Mandate and the Strategies of the Inspectors-General

The legislative mandate launched the OIGs, but White House interests in using the OIGs became influential in shaping the enterprise as the administrative tasks of building the organizations and structuring their relationships to other executive branch agencies (such as the Department of Justice, the Office of Management and Budget, the offices of administration and management in the departments and the various program offices) came to the fore. Both Presidents Carter and Reagan established special structures to provide leadership to the Inspectors-General. The Presidents differed, however, in their aims and emphases for the enterprise.

Presidential Mandates for the Offices of Inspectors-General

Although President Carter initially opposed the legislation establishing the OIGs, once it passed he embraced it enthusiastically. He established an interagency council called the Executive Group to Combat Fraud and Waste.[63] It was chaired by the Deputy Attorney General, and its members included the twelve statutory OIGs, the Deputy Director of the Office of Personnel Management, and the nonstatutory OIGs from the Departments of Defense, State, and Treasury. It was staffed by officials from the Office of Management and Budget (OMB), and it included representatives from the Federal Bureau of Investigation, the Internal Revenue Service, and the Postal Inspection Service.[64] The essential tasks of this group were those of all high-level, interdepartmental groups: to provide a special channel for an important new enterprise to identify problems and advocate for resources and influence; to allow the President and OMB to keep an eye on its operations; to work on issues that cut across agencies; and to learn from the subordinate agencies, encourage them, and share the credit for individual initiatives launched by the participating groups.

Compared with the Carter Administration's efforts in other areas such as drug abuse prevention or, indeed, to President Reagan's subsequent efforts with the OIGs, the support given by Carter to the OIGs was a bit tepid. The interagency council was kept out of the main channel of command to the White House and OMB.[65] Its advocacy of additional resources for the OIGs was halfhearted, though from FY 1980 to FY 1981 the resources devoted to the OIGs increased by 5 percent in the number of positions and 12 percent in overall spending.[66] The Executive Group's principal initiatives were the establishment of "whistleblower hot lines" for use by agency employees, improved procedures governing agency use of consultants, and purchase and control of furniture.[67]

While the broad domain of OIG activities was recognized and maintained by Carter's Executive Group, the primary role assigned to the OIGs was to attack fraud and waste through improved criminal investigations. That this was Carter's priority was signaled by his choosing the Deputy Attorney General to chair the Executive Group. The effective control of white collar crime was at that time one of the Department of Justice's highest priorities, and defrauding government programs was one of the highest priorities within the white collar crime program.[68] The inclusion of the FBI and other relevant investigative agencies in the group, and the establishment of the hot lines reinforced Carter's emphasis on investigations and prosecutions, as did the fact that appointees to the post of Inspector-General were heavily drawn from the ranks of prosecutors and lawyers rather than auditors or accountants. This function was also consistent with the spirit of the legislative history that lay behind the Inspectors-General Act of 1978.

Whatever the long-run potential of this group, its operations ended abruptly with the election of Ronald Reagan. On January 20, 1981—his inauguration day—President Reagan abruptly fired all the existing Inspectors-General, explaining to Congress and the American public that this group was insufficiently zealous in rooting out fraud, waste, and abuse.[69] Many in the IG community thought that Reagan's intervention would end the IG movement. But Reagan and OMB moved quickly not only to re-establish the enterprise, but also to elevate its importance and provide it with a distinctive Reagan Administration imprint.

The President quickly appointed people to fill the vacant IG posts. About half of those who were fired were rehired, but moved to different agencies.[70] Reagan added others, but in filling the positions he drew more from the ranks of auditors and investigators than from the ranks of lawyers and prosecutors.[71] His Press Secretary, James Brady, explained that the administration wanted IGs who were "meaner than junkyard dogs."[72] Moreover, through an Executive Order, the President established an entity called the President's Council on Integrity and Efficiency (PCIE).[73] This group was chaired by the Deputy Director of OMB, Edwin L. Harper. It included all those in Carter's Executive Group to Combat Fraud and Waste, with the following exceptions: (1) the Deputy Attorney General remained on the Council, but was removed from the chairmanship; (2) representation from the Office of Personnel Management was upgraded from the Deputy Director to the Director; (3) the representatives from IRS and the Postal Service were dropped; and (4) four new statutory IGs were added to the group.[74]

In establishing the Council, Reagan indicated that it was to be simply one element of a broader OMB-led strategy to strengthen management throughout the government. As time went on, the other elements of this strategy were put into place. One was the establishment of a Cabinet Council on Administration and Management as one of the five or six key policy-making entities reporting to the White House. A second was the launching of the President's Commission on Cost Control led by private sector executive J. Peter Grade. A third was the establishment of an informal working group of Assistant Secretaries for Administration and Management, so that they could have the same kind of status that was afforded to OIGs. All of these elements were wrapped together in a program originally called "Reform '84," and then, as 1984 approached and as prospects for Reagan's reelection brightened, the name was changed to "Reform '88."[75] This program became the central management initiative of OMB, led originally by Ed Harper, an OMB executive, and eventually taken over by Joe Wright, another OMB official.

Inevitably, the PCIE became a stronger organizational entity than Carter's Executive Group. Since it was created by an Executive Order and had close ties to the White House through OMB and the Cabinet Council on Administration and Management, its standing with all executive branch agencies was strengthened. In addition, President Reagan kept pointing to his efforts to control fraud, waste, and abuse as a central component of his plans for lowering taxes and avoiding major deficits, despite the fact that no one really thought there was enough money to be squeezed out of controlling fraud, waste, and abuse to produce more than a token response to the large budget deficits that were accumulating. And, finally, since OMB was riding high in the administration, its sponsorship of the PCIE made the group even more powerful. As one IG exulted, "the PCIE is the best thing that ever happened to us."[76]

The focus of Reagan's PCIE is quite different from Carter's Executive Group. At the outset, its rhetoric was more extreme than Carter's Executive Group and quite narrowly focused on fraud and abuse. Publications from the PCIE prominently quote Reagan's charge to the organization: "to follow every lead, root out every incompetent, and prosecute any crook we find who's cheating the people of this nation."[77] Consistent with this spirit, the PCIE's initial reports emphasized quantitative achievements in three areas: the detection of fraud, waste, and abuse; the recovery of losses through fines of individuals and audit resolutions; and the punishment of those responsible. These elements continue to constitute the core of the PCIE reports.

Increasingly, however, as (1) doubts were raised by GAO and others about the accuracy of the numbers, (2) mistakes were disclosed that were particularly embarrassing to a group committed to accurate accounting, and (3) the PCIE and the Inspectors-General really got down to work, the PCIE began to emphasize the role of cost avoidances and cost savings that could be achieved through the redesign of administrative procedures and preventive efforts rather than the elimination of fraud. Indeed, as the PCIE sought to discover ways to maximize the impact of the OIGs on the size of the deficit, it began with efforts to prosecute thieves and recover cash and has moved from these to designing preventive systems. As a recent report states:

> Use of audit and investigative techniques as a deterrent to potential fraud and abuse is not new. The manner in which these techniques are applied and the organizational structure used to bring them to bear on problems have changed dramatically. *The auditor's and investigator's roles have evolved to provide advice, before the fact, on how best to attain stronger, less vulnerable systems and controls.* [Emphasis added.][78]

Consistent with this spirit, the PCIE has established a special Prevention Committee and has given special attention to developing and widely disseminating "computer matching systems."[79]

Like the Carter Executive Group before it, however, Reagan's PCIE has found it difficult to produce much of an increase in the total volume of resources devoted to investigation, audit, or systems improvements. Resources devoted to the OIGs have not grown by any substantial amount over the last five years. Instead, the PCIE seems to be encouraging the more effective use of existing resources by shifting some of the burden for auditing and systems design onto client organizations and management; by targeting investigations, audits, and administrative improvements in the programs that seem most vulnerable; and by encouraging greater reliance on computer technologies in the conduct of audits, as well as in the operations of government programs.

In sum, the Reagan Administration has created a great deal of room for the OIGs. It has made the OIGs important and influential. It has guarded them against substantial losses, although it has not dramatically increased their activities. It has kept the pressure on them to perform in traditional areas of prosecutions, debt collections, and audit resolutions, but has also acknowledged the importance of broader prevention activities and tried to develop measures of the value of these activities. Exactly how these opportunities are being utilized, however, depends ultimately on the strategies and leadership of the IGs themselves.

The Organizational Strategies of the Inspectors-General

The IGs in both the Carter and Reagan Administrations made choices about the purposes and operating styles of their organizations. They decided how the Offices would be organized and staffed, what their central work would be, how they would manage their relationships with the program managers and with the external world of Congress, the press, and the special units created by Presidents Carter and Reagan to assist in their development. Of course, the OIGs received guidance on how to make these choices from both legislative and presidential mandates. But the choices were also influenced significantly by the interests and capabilities of the investigative and audit staffs the specific IGs inherited; by the particular histories, public images, and problems of the organizations they joined; by the backgrounds and orientations of the IGs themselves; and perhaps, most important, by the accumulation of experience with the OIG function. Consequently, examination of the strategies of the Inspectors-General reveals, first, significant commonalities among the OIGs and over time. But a closer look reveals some important differences among the OIGs that seem determined primarily by the specific organizations to which they belong. And a still closer look reveals a fairly natural evolution of the concept of the OIGs so that the cross-sectional differences among OIGs seem to be produced not only by differences in the particular organizations, but also by differences in the amount of experience the organizations have had with the OIG function.

ORGANIZING AND STAFFING THE OFFICES

Perhaps the most important decision about the organization and staffing of the OIGs was made by Congress. Although Congress seemed interested in producing some operational coordination between investigators and auditors and in using the information they developed to design systems that could prevent fraud, waste, and abuse or promote efficiency, it based the OIGs on preserving the disciplines of investigation and audit. Indeed, Congress wrote into the statute a requirement that each Inspector-General establish an Assistant Inspector-General for Investigation and an Assistant Inspector-General for Audit.[80] The law seemed to preclude organizing investigators and auditors around specific programs or developing and training "audigators" who combined the skills of both professions.

To a degree, the decision to preserve the investigative and audit functions intact created a leadership problem for first-generation IGs. The IG often arrived on the job to find heads of investigative and audit units already in place. Often, these officials had aspired to the IG position and viewed the appearance of presidential appointees not only as a personal insult, but also as a serious threat to their professional integrity and that of their staff. They were by no means sure that they could rely on the new IGs to preserve the autonomy and independence that the Inspector-General Act promised.

Reaction to this situation varied widely. Some IGs, like Tom Morris at HEW and Kurt Muellenberg at the General Services Administration (GSA), quickly hired the people they needed to accomplish what they perceived to be their mission.[81] Their initial instinct seems to have been to make as few changes as possible in the organizational units they inherited and to concentrate on adding new dimensions as needed. Morris, in fact, declined to consolidate all of HEW's investigators within his office, realizing that to do so would invite interoffice hostility among the investigative units at a time when he considered other problems more important. Congress was critical of him for this omission.[82] Muellenberg was soon forced to confront his AIGs who had taken issue with the way he organized and ran the office. He transferred the AIG for Investigations out of the Office and hired a replacement from outside the IG community. The repercussions of this decisive if somewhat belated move caused Muellenberg to spend an inordinate amount of time defending his actions before Congress and the press.[83]

Although other IGs made organization and hiring their first priority, they did not fare well either. Marjorie Knowles took the IG position at the Department of Labor (DOL) with the agreement that she would stay long enough to accomplish these tasks. When she left a year later she had spent most of her time in office hiring top-level staff and establishing a third AIG unit for Loss Analysis and Prevention.[84] At this writing, most of these people have been dispersed and the new unit has been dismantled. In addition, Knowles's former deputy and successor, Ron Goldstock, says he spent half his time dealing with personnel problems, including law suits and internal criminal investigations, some of which resulted from efforts to rid the organization of people considered incompetent.[85] At USDA, McBride had a head start on the other statutory IGs and managed to detail both the head of audit and the head of investigation to jobs outside OIG. The people he wanted as AIGs were therefore serving as Acting AIGs, and for long periods the staff was uncertain who ultimately would be in charge.[86]

For every Inspector-General, filling the two pivotal AIG positions was critical because it was only through these officials that an IG could command the bulk of his/her resources. Loyalty and the ability to translate the IGs' understanding of the mission into programmatic action are qualities which any IG would consider essential in filling AIG jobs. Furthermore, in order to implement IG policy, the AIGs had to be able to secure the respect and loyalty of the auditors and investigators.

Obviously, these requirements are not unique to IG offices, but they may be more difficult to fulfill in the IG setting. First, as mentioned earlier, some heads of audit and investigation offices were disappointed contenders for IG positions. Second, many of them were accustomed to operating in a somewhat autonomous fashion, despite the fact that they reported to an Assistant Secretary or a program manager. The essence of audit and investigation is objectivity and, although managers may have wrongly compromised these functions on occasion, it has been generally accepted that these functions operate at arm's length from programs and from political direction. The spirit of independence runs high among these professionals, so they were predictably wary of taking direction from a presidentially appointed IG. In short, they preferred an IG to be their champion, to take their conclusions to the highest levels of management and force acceptance of them, rather than to negotiate with program managers. Too often, the negotiation process seemed like compromise and capitulation.

Although the Offices of Audit and Investigation often shared such traits, they are not alike in most respects. In fact, one of the most intractable problems for IGs is how to manage the natural tensions that exist between the investigation and audit functions and to get them to work together. They are both fact-finding functions, but their professions are peopled by very different personality types. The derogatory characterization of investigators as "gumshoes" and auditors as "eye shades" is nowhere more prevalent than among the chief components of OIG itself. Rivalry for the attention of the IG and for resources heightens this effect.

These jealousies could ordinarily be resolved satisfactorily at the AIG level where close contact eventually leads to cooperation. But it is much more difficult to facilitate these relationships among operational units. The task of investigators and auditors is to develop concrete facts about an organization's operation, which means that they must be in immediate contact with far-flung field offices and that they are often traveling to and from these offices. Thus, it is not unusual to visit an IG field office and find only the manager and support staff. As one IG remarked, "an IG's office *is* people who travel."[87] The far-flung field offices and frequent travel make it difficult for central managers in Washington to communicate important changes in attitudes or subtle shifts in policy. To solve this problem, McBride at USDA, for example, chose to visit most IG field offices, and brought people in from the field to communicate information on the Office of Economic Opportunity (OEO) and affirmative action policies.[88] In order to bring audit and investigation into a working relationship, he required that they be housed in the same building but remarked that as far as results were concerned, "it was like leading a horse to water."[89]

The continuing investigation and audit activities of the existing organizational units provide the core activities and functions of the OIGs. To the extent that these activities and the increasing importance of investigation and audit as a function give the OIGs an important task and *raison d'être,* investigation and audit are real assets for the IGs. But their existence also creates some problems for IGs who want to justify public enthusiasm for their enterprises and solidify their position by making important contributions to the effective prevention of fraud, waste, and abuse, and the promotion of efficiency.

One major problem is an embarrassing gap between the potential size of the investigation and audit universe and the real capacity of the IG offices. The gap is particularly wide in the area of audit in which rather precise calculations of the difference between the desired level of audits and actual capacity to produce the audits could be made. In the CETA Program, for example, a legislative mandate called for an annual audit of about 450 "prime sponsors" who operated the program for the federal government across the country. The OIG at DOL could do no more than half of these audits in any given year.[90]

Given that the IGs were unsuccessful in gaining any dramatic increase in resources, they relied on a variety of devices to try to close the gaps in investigative and audit coverage. One tactic was to turn the audit responsibility over to others. Thus, the "prime sponsors" in CETA were encouraged to procure audits on their own.[91] The IG at DOL provided technical assistance and oversight of these commercial audits, but did not conduct them. A second tactic was to try to increase the efficiency with which investigation and audit resources were used by focusing them on programs that were judged to be the most vulnerable to corruption.[92] Thus, investigators reduced their reliance on hot lines and shifted to proactive investigations and auditors focused on the programs that were widely suspected to be vulnerable to fraud, waste, and abuse. Indeed, many IGs established separate "planning and evaluation" units to help set priorities.[93] They also took advantage of an OMB requirement that managers conduct "vulnerability assessments" of their programs.[94] A third tactic, which is becoming particularly popular with second-generation IGs, was to improve the efficiency of investigations and audits by relying more heavily on computers to support program operations and to facilitate auditing.[95] Despite these efforts, the "audit gap" remains embarrassing—in particular to organizations that demand responsible performance from others.

A second major problem associated with organizing the Offices of Inspectors-General around the tasks of investigation and audit is that it has been difficult to go beyond these separate functions to achieve short-run operational coordination, or longer-run benefits associated with using the experience developed in investigations and audits to design administrative procedures that make the programs less vulnerable to fraud, waste, and abuse or promote efficiency. In a sense, these core activities create a drag on the IGs' efforts to exploit the broader opportunities to contribute to government integrity and efficiency that the Congress and both Presidents hoped to promote.

Both first- and second-generation IGs have tried to deliver on these aspirations by developing new capabilities in their organizations. The first-generation IGs we interviewed sought to integrate investigation and audit and to move them from detection of fraud and abuse to prevention—and ultimately to the promotion of efficiency through two different means. First, the IGs established an additional section, usually headed by an AIG, to do analytic work related to defining and carrying out these broader, more integrated objectives.[96] GSA had its Special Projects Staff; DOL had its Office of Loss Analysis and Prevention; USDA had its Planning, Review and Evaluation Section; and HEW had an Assistant Inspector General for Health Care and Systems Review. Second, to staff these special hybrid offices, the IGs hired people with expertise in law, program evaluation, computer sciences, and management.

Although these special units were credited with some exceptionally valuable work—usually in the areas of intensive investigations of particularly complex problems, the strategic assessment of the magnitude and location of major problems, or the design of new prevention mechanisms—they eventually all came to be considered dysfunctional. The units in GSA and DOL have been completely dismantled,[97] and those in USDA and HHS (formerly HEW) have been extensively reorganized.[98]

One factor contributing to the temporary demise of these offices created by the first-generation IGs was the bureaucratic difficulty of establishing secure jobs and career paths for those who joined a hybrid office. The IGs found it difficult to establish a Civil Service classification for positions such as "loss prevention analyst" that recognized the contributions of computer and management specialists to the IG enterprise. Similarly, the General Counsels of the various departments resisted the development of positions for attorneys in the IG Offices and resisted the transfer or hiring of their people to work in these jobs. Even for traditional professions, technical problems arose. Investigators in the 1811 series could not be detailed to work on other than criminal investigations for more than a certain amount of time without jeopardizing certain retirement rights. Auditors, unlike those who work for GAO, were required to have a requisite number of academic credits in financial accounting.

Following a brief hiatus, second-generation IGs have also begun to develop organizational units and approaches that go beyond traditional investigation and audit activities. The second-generation IGs describe the function to be performed as "inspections" rather than "investigations" or "audits."[99] In June 1983 a GAO investigation of IG offices found that only 6 of the

16 statutory IG offices had any organizational entity or resources committed to tasks other than traditional investigations and audits.[100] A more recent survey by the Prevention Committee of the PCIE found that 11 of the 17 statutory offices now have separate units or activities devoted to "inspections."[101]

Because this function is new, its tasks, procedures, and quantitative effects are unclear. What is clear is that this function represents the efforts of second-generation IGs to close the "audit gap" and to make a contribution to government operations that goes beyond traditional investigation and audit. Inspections are more flexible in methodology than investigations and audits. They reach for a closer involvement with program managers, and they emphasize evaluations of the efficiency of operations over compliance with laws and regulations or the effectiveness of techniques to detect and prevent fraud, waste, and abuse. Their flexibility allows the Inspectors-General to use them to extend audit coverage to areas they could not reach with traditional methods, and, in particular, to make a contribution to programs early in their development before they have enough operating experience to justify investigations and audits.[102]

In its ambitions to go beyond investigations and audits, and in its flexibility, the "inspection" function is the inheritor of the tradition of special offices established by the first-generation IGs. The "inspection" function, however, seems to be centered not on special efforts to detect fraud and abuse, nor on the design of preventive systems, but instead on the assessment of efficiency and effectiveness. Moreover, they are less concerned with planning and evaluating IG operations than they are with carrying out a new IG function. In both respects, these functions seem even less traditional than the innovations introduced by the first generation. No doubt, the license granted by the PCIE has emboldened the second-generation IGs to move in this direction. But much of the thrust comes from the second-generation IGs themselves, who seem much more committed to preventing fraud and abuse and promoting efficiency than the first-generation IGs, and who are reaching out for a broader consultative relation with managers.[103]

This commitment differs from agency to agency, of course. In general the longer an IG has worked in an agency, and the farther an agency is from scandals involving fraud, the more likely it is that the IG will think in terms of the prevention of fraud and the promotion of efficiency, and the more satisfactory will be his relations with management.

This is revealed clearly in Table 2, which offers some summary views of the strategies adopted by the IGs. Among first-generation IGs, the strategies of those in HEW and USDA were the broadest because they had the longest operating experience. In DOL and GSA, agencies with no IG tradition and recent histories of scandal, the strategies were narrower and relations with managers worse. By the second generation, these differences were less marked though by no means entirely eliminated. In the second generation everyone seems committed to the broader mission.

The fact that such organizational problems all but overwhelmed the first-generation IGs comes as no surprise to Charles Dempsey, Inspector-General at HUD, who noted that it took five years for Les Condon, whom he described as possibly "the best IG ever," to pull the nonstatutory IG office together at HUD.[104] He adds that Condon had the full support of management and none of the political complexities to which the more recent statutory IGs fell heir. Bryan Mitchell, Deputy Inspector-General at HEW (later HHS) who has been instrumental since 1975 in developing that office, noted that important organizational changes, including the consolidation of investigative resources which have been on the drawing board for four years at HHS (formerly HEW), are only now being implemented.[105] However, he, too, believes that IGs should resign themselves to the fact that establishing a new government function takes a number of years. Another IG, not included in the interview samples, remarked that personnel problems and reorganization are especially difficult for IGs and other managers who come from outside government and are unfamiliar with the system.[106]

DEFINING THE WORK

How IGs define the mission of their office seems to depend on a number of factors: (1) their understanding of congressional intent in the Inspector-General Act, (2) direction from higher-level IG "coordinating groups" that were established in both Carter and Reagan Administrations, (3) the expectations of the agency head, (4) the particular problems of their agency, and (5) their professional background.

Table 2 The Strategies of Inspectors-General

	Primary Focus and Thrust	Internal Management Problems	Relations with Program Management
First Generation			
Dempsey (HUD)	To use audit and investigation to produce information for prevention of fraud, waste, and abuse; to advise management on loss prevention	Few problems due to long history of office	Actively cooperative
McBride (USDA)	To prevent and detect fraud; to recoup dollar losses; to assume integrity of federal employees	Changes in mid management/ creation of priority-setting office; low-level morale problem	Mostly cooperative; press leaks and releases created some suspicions
Morris (HHS)	To use audit and investigation to produce information for prevention of fraud, waste, and abuse; to advise management on loss prevention	Few problems: predominantly audit organization	Strong support from top management
Knowles (DOL)	To prevent loss; to emphasize importance of legislative changes as well as management reform	Major problems: hiring senior staff; competence of lower levels	Difficult due to incompetence of auditors and investigators

Muellenberg (GSA)	To investigate proactively; to promote efficiency	Major problems	Difficult due to leaks, attitudes of auditors, and fears of management
Second Generation			
Dempsey (HUD)	Unchanged from above	Unchanged from above	Improved; Reagan election has increased management's interest and receptivity
Graziano (USDA)	To prevent fraud, waste, and abuse; to promote efficiency	Setting up staff to work with management on vulnerability assessments	Very good; managers are responsive
Kusserow (HHS)	To prevent fraud and abuse; to advise management on systems to prevent losses	Priority setting	Managers are very responsive
McBride (DOL)	To move to include "reduced inefficiency" as objective; to examine whole operation of program	Many problems resolved	Substantially improved; goal is to "educate" management; finds managers responsive
Sikon (GSA)	To audit proactively	Problems lessened, but not resolved	Improving, but still difficult

The professional background of each appointee would obviously affect the skills he or she brought to the job. In addition, however, the relative weight of professions represented in the IG corps conveys the administration's perception of what IGs should do. While the original Carter appointees represented a number of fields, almost half of them were lawyers (Muellenberg, McBride, Knowles, Bass, Freeman, Tied, Boucher). Among the IGs reappointed by Reagan, the lawyers and especially the former prosecutors were noticeably absent (Muellenberg at GSA; Lowe, Acting IG at HHS; Goldstock, Acting IG at DOL). This seems to have signaled a lessening of concern about the detection of fraud and abuse and a heightened emphasis on the prevention of fraud and the promotion of efficiency.

REDUCING FRAUD AND ABUSE VERSUS PROMOTING EFFICIENCY. Whatever the true motivation of each president was in this respect, Carter IG appointees did seem to see law enforcement against fraud and abuse as a major goal. As noted above, they were reinforced in this belief by the fact that Carter's Executive Group to Combat Fraud and Waste was chaired by the Deputy Attorney General and met at the Department of Justice. This focus resonated most strongly with agencies which had recently been rocked by scandals and whose administrators wanted an IG who could take the problems of fraud, kickbacks, and corruption off their hands.

Perhaps the best example of this phenomenon was Kurt Muellenberg, IG at the GSA. He was the first IG appointee under the 1978 Act, undoubtedly because GSA was at the time the most visibly scandal-ridden agency of the federal government. Muellenberg assumed that his chief qualification for the job was his career-long service in the Criminal Division of DOJ. Therefore, he felt that he was expected to set up a primarily law enforcement/ crime prevention office.[107]

The Reagan-appointed IGs, however, are predominantly non-lawyers; a larger percentage of them are career civil servants than were the Carter IGs. In fact, all of the first-generation IGs rehired by Reagan were career people with significant government experience, and all of the noncareer appointees were let go. To the extent that this shift was intentional, it may indicate a desire to guarantee a nonpartisan IG corps or it may simply signify a preference for professionals with a great deal of experience in federal government operations.

At least one IG says that audit managers make the best IGs because they are well grounded in government procedures and programs. But the question of which profession produces the "best" IGs begs the question of what the IG is supposed to do. Prosecutors are apt to be best at rooting out fraud and corruption while auditors are more likely to excel at cutting costs. In all likelihood, the best IGs are those who can not only balance investigations with audits, but also lead both into a more cooperative, mutually supportive relationship with program managers.

The activities of the current IGs are coordinated through the President's Council on Integrity and Efficiency (PCIE) based in OMB. The Criminal Division of DOJ is not even represented. OMB has made clear its preference for IG concentration on *management* issues and for IGs to work in a cooperative mode with managers. The second-generation IGs have responded to this change.

DETECTION VERSUS PREVENTION. The goal of the OIGs is commonly expressed as "ferreting out fraud, waste, and abuse." This terminology reflects the belief that the Inspector-General's duty is to detect and expose problems. First-generation IGs initially concentrated on the detection function, developing techniques such as computer matching programs to identify possible violators for investigative action.[108] Investigators under Muellenberg at GSA launched "proactive" efforts rather than waiting for suspected fraud and abuse to be reported to them.[109] At USDA investigators mounted sophisticated "sting" operations to identify food stamp traffickers.[110] Such activity presumably convinced the public that the IGs were effective watchdogs and possibly deterred would-be offenders. It also had the potential for alienating managers.

Furthermore, increased detection of crime and abuse gives rise to several other problems. First, it produces demand for more investigative and prosecutorial resources. Although many IGs were able to hire additional investigators to deal with the increased case load, this augmentation of IG resources began to threaten the FBI and caused rivalry between the Bureau and OIG agents for the attention of federal prosecutors.[111] In addition, little was done by DOJ to increase the capacity of U.S. Attorneys to deal with increased IG referrals. Consequently, investigative time was wasted developing cases that ultimately would be declined.

IGs with experience as prosecutors dealt with this dilemma in different ways. McBride insisted that his agents refer cases to U.S. Attorney offices at an early stage to get a reading on whether the case would be prosecuted if investigation confirmed the allegations and to seek guidance from the prosecutor.[112] Muellenberg, on the other hand, hired lawyers to direct special proactive investigations, and he referred to a special DOJ task force only those cases deemed to merit prosecution. He believes that IGs, because of their audit capacity and location within the agency, are ideally situated to detect problems that would otherwise go undetected. This is the OIGs, chief advantage over the FBI.[113] Goldstock developed a somewhat skeptical attitude toward detection, investigation, and prosecution altogether, turning instead to prevention as the proper IG approach.[114]

Richard Kusserow from HHS, a second-generation IG and a former FBI agent, also rejects the pursuit of indictments and convictions as the IG's primary goal. He believes that these will come naturally as a result of continuing investigative capacities. The mandate to *detect* fraud and abuse, he holds, is related primarily to discovering how to *prevent* those problems. In support of his opinion he argues that as prevention measures improve there will be less fraud and abuse and, therefore, fewer indictments, making an increase in the latter a poor indicator of an IG's success.[115] Of course, it is not uncommon for law enforcement agencies to be in this position since crime prevention is an accepted strategy for police departments and other agencies. However, the IGs apparently have the option to declare prevention as their principal approach, to subordinate the detection function, and to relegate investigation to the FBI or other agencies.

This, in fact, appears to be the trend. One IG said that for every 20 people he could hire, 19 would be auditors and one an investigator.[116] The second-generation IGs we interviewed all emphasized the importance of prevention over detection and investigation. For example, John V. Graziano, a former AIG for Investigations, stressed the primacy of managerial tactics to decrease the vulnerability of the Food Stamp Program and downplayed USDA's long-standing efforts to apprehend traffickers.[117] McBride, who as IG at USDA was very supportive of investigative activity, took a different tack as the Reagan Administration IG at DOL. There he concentrated almost exclusively on systems problems and argued that poor management and program delivery systems were at the root of most fraud, waste, and abuse.[118]

While this proposition is certainly defensible, it does raise questions about the role of the IG in management improvement. How the IG's overriding concern about fraud, waste, and abuse prevention as opposed to other legitimate managerial objectives affects that role is a central concern of this study.

INTERNAL FOCUS VERSUS EXTERNAL FOCUS. The 1976 legislation creating an Inspector-General at HEW was passed largely because of abuses resulting from poor administration of programs at the state and local level. Recognizing this, Secretary Joseph P. Califano personally launched a meeting of state administrators to consider alternative ways of controlling the problem.[119] Similarly, McBride targeted meetings of Food Stamp Administrators as opportunities for educating them about ways to reduce fraud and waste.[120] This strategy may or may not be effective in terms of reducing program abuse, but it certainly is less alienating to federal program managers than one which focuses on flaws in the federal management of the program.

Nevertheless, there has been an observable shift in emphasis among IGs away from external audit and toward internal management audits. Under OMB "Circular A-102 Attachment P," audits are provided by the states. With respect to audits of external units, OIGs are increasingly overseeing audits performed by private contractors rather than doing the work themselves. Instead, federal auditors are being directed by IGs toward *internal* management issues. Dempsey says that any IG who is not devoting half of his/her audit resources to internal problems is not doing the job Congress intended.[121]

Again, this tendency of IGs to look at program management systems rather than detect losses and abuses at the delivery point may bring IG activity into conflict with the responsibilities of managers. However, the most experienced IGs seem to be learning that establishing claims against state and local entities for losses sustained in the administration of programs is sometimes futile except that it may give the federal government the leverage needed to insist on more secure administrative systems. They also realize that prosecution of private parties for fraud or abuse is seldom cost-effective. Their conclusion that losses can most effectively be cut by changing the way programs are delivered is a natural one. The question remains: what can the IG contribute to this effort?

RELATIONSHIP WITH MANAGEMENT

The major issue in defining the proper relationship between the IG and management is whether it is that of friends, foes, or professional colleagues. The traditional stance of auditors and investigators has been objective, or even adversarial, toward managers. They did not want to talk to managers too much lest the conversations compromise the objectivity of their investigations and audits. In fact, one of the reasons for the original Inspector-General Act was to assure a stronger position for audits and investigations in confrontations with managers. Congress apparently saw the IG as the champion of certain values which would naturally be resisted by program officials but under the Act would be reinforced by congressional attention.

Most of the first-generation IGs we interviewed found significant antipathy between auditors and managers when they took office. Dempsey (HUD) says that the reason is mainly that auditors forget that "their role is advisory" and they try to "dictate to management." He also acknowledges that managers have a reasonable fear of being "blindsided" by audit.[122] Muellenberg (GSA) and Sikon (GSA) report that the audit-management relationship in their agencies could not have been worse, owing to the unauthorized release of draft audit reports to the press.[123] "Leaks" of draft audit findings before management has replied on the record violates the GAO standards which the Inspectors-General Act requires IGs to obey. Sikon says, "If I've missed something during an audit and they [management] bring it up, they are doing me a favor—not a disservice. If there's any disservice maybe I'm doing it to them."[124] When an agency is already under fire for fraud and mismanagement as GSA was, the press's temptation to use audit findings which have not been validated is great and the result is especially damaging.

Another problem in the audit-management interface has been the accuracy of audit findings. Goldstock (DOL) identifies this as a critical problem which undermines OIG credibility.[125] The questioned reliability of audit figures at GSA was aggravated by the "leaks" which robbed managers of their right to dispute findings. A similar situation occurred at USDA during McBride's term there. Statistical sampling and projection of results for a national food delivery program produced huge loss figures, which were disputed by the agency. While the IG worked with agency managers and technicians to verify the numbers (which turned out to be grossly distorted by a computer programming mistake), auditors released the figures to a congressional committee.[126] Such mistakes are usually discovered by management and can be corrected in the final audit report, but the credibility of audit is diminished by the error. Of course, the integrity of the audit process is also jeopardized when the problem of audit error is compounded by premature release. Ironically, what is at stake in these situations is the accountability of the audit process, and accountability is precisely the value which auditors are supposed to ensure.

Goldstock (DOL) acknowledged this antagonism between audit and management when he coined the term "IG tolerance" to describe the reaction of managers to IG recommendations.[127] As Dempsey points out, auditors cannot "dictate to management." Even when a strong IG backs up audit recommendations and brings them to the attention of the agency head and Congress, managers still make the decisions.[128] Goldstock says that "there is no point in coming up with recommendations which management will never accept."[129] To illustrate how an IG could avoid a counterproductive, adversarial relationship, Goldstock tells of one case in which his office had done a comprehensive analysis of a major program that culminated in 100 recommendations. Anticipating great resistance on the part of the program, the IG report characterized the analysis as having been undertaken at the request of the program's manager, which was not the case. This face-saving technique put the IG in the posture of an ally rather than an adversary.[130] Sikon (GSA) echoes this message when he says he tells auditors "to give managers a recommendation that is realistic and within their resources to implement. 'Textbook solutions' may lead to irreconcilable conflict."[131] All IGs interviewed believed that they should use a carrot rather than a stick whenever possible in dealing with program managers. They also felt that an IG could not perform successfully without the support of the agency head.

The desire of IGs to consider themselves members of the management team in the promotion of economy and efficiency has an important and unexpected effect: the IGs often alienate their own auditors and investigators who think that politically motivated IGs have "sold out" to management. Sikon found that GSA auditors had been trained by the former AIG not to talk to managers because to do so "prostituted the IG's independence."[132] Dempsey has also noted the preoccupation with independence on the part of auditors. He believes that IG independence is an important principle in creating credibility and access, but "insisting on independence is begging for trouble." He is adamant that IGs cannot "take cheap shots," and he does not approve of IGs publicizing their findings because the embarrassment it causes managers is alienating to managers and counterproductive to the IG's working relationships with them.[133] Because it is difficult to dissuade many auditors from the traditional attitudes, Dempsey feels IGs must be aggressive in this regard, using promotion and transfers where necessary to bring the organization into line.[134]

McBride found that at USDA he had to use both a carrot and a stick, depending on the program. The Food Stamp Program had powerful enemies in Congress and was closely watched by the press, so its managers were interested in following IG advice about reducing its vulnerability to fraud, waste, and abuse. On the other hand, the Farmers Home Administration was a political favorite for its ability to make large loans for many diverse purposes. Congress was more interested in getting funds quickly to their constituents than in improving loan-making procedures and increasing the servicing of the loans. The IG had little leverage in the latter situation beyond warning the Secretary of potential embarrassment.[135]

Under the Reagan Administration, a noticeable change has taken place, according to McBride. The White House has sent clear messages to top-level managers to reverse what McBride calls "the prior domination of concern for program delivery at the expense of any notion of accountability or a fiduciary role with regard to those expenditures."[136] Even before McBride came aboard as IG at DOL, the Assistant Secretaries had given program controls a very high priority. This "top down" education of managers is clearly more effective than the same antifraud, waste, and abuses messages delivered by an IG. McBride also believes that IG initiatives are more effective when they are introduced across agencies and with some "machinery" like the debt collection project.[137] Such projects have the impetus that can only come from high-level presidential and OMB interest.

Another example of how a combined IG and management approach can produce dramatic results is revealed by the significant decrease or elimination of unresolved audits under the Reagan Administration. Dempsey claims an enormous backlog was dissipated simply because President Reagan asked the cabinet at a meeting what they were doing about this problem. When the cabinet secretaries returned to their departments they made the resolution of outstanding audits a high priority.[138]

Dempsey lauds the move of the IG coordinating body (PCIE) out of DOJ, away from the emphasis on criminal work and into OMB. He also praises the management side of OMB and its ability to build up the expertise of the IGs and to coordinate joint IG projects.[139] There seems to be agreement among IGs that the PCIE has been a strong unifying force which has made the IGs important instruments in this administration's management plans.

A most important aspect of IG relationships with management emerged from the interviews, although it is a concern usually expressed by managers. IGs maintain that Congress took away from managers two important tools (audit and investigation) and gave them to the IGs. Morris (HHS) says he has heard managers say, in effect, that "the IG has taken the ball away from me in terms of management improvement."[140] Now managers must rely on the IG to secure basic information about the character of their operations. Goldstock believes that managers are perfectly positioned to detect fraud, abuse, and waste in their programs, but by taking away their internal audit capacity Congress gave them "an absolute out."[141] He thinks managers should be primarily responsible for combating fraud, waste, and abuse and that the IG should simply monitor those efforts.

Although this issue can be intelligently argued either way, it is clear that the framers of the Inspector-General Act believed that managers were not making good use of their audit and investigative capacity. Transferring those resources to an official with no program responsibilities, and giving that individual access to the highest level of the executive and legislative branches, is precisely the purpose of the legislation. The fact that managers feel deprived of tools, subject to undue criticism, and answerable to a potentially hostile force was foreseeable and probably intended.

The original symbol of the IG was the watchdog, which is not the sort of mascot needed in a community of trust. When the Reagan Administration said that it would hire IGs who are meaner than junkyard dogs, the symbol became more aggressive and offensive. Nonetheless, it appears that, on the contrary, the IGs are moving closer to the canine image of man's best friend as they seek to develop more cooperative working relationships with managers.

Part IV Evaluating the Impact of the Offices of Inspectors-General

The Inspectors-General are charged broadly with improving the accountability, and therefore the performance, of government. To evaluate them, then, is to ask how well they have achieved these purposes. As noted above, our judgments must be considered preliminary. Since the institutions are still developing, and since we had only limited capacities to observe the effects, our conclusions must be held contingently until more experience accumulates and better evidence on effects comes along. In the parlance of OIGs, then, our exploration should be considered an "inspection" of a new program that provides the basis for a discussion with the program's managers. It is not an "investigation" or "audit" that comes to firm conclusions, assigns praise and criticism, and points an unambiguous path toward improvement.

In making our "inspection" of the OIGs, we can begin with an examination of the internal operations of the program itself. We can look at how it is organized and staffed, the resources that are committed, the procedures that are utilized, and the articulated aspirations of the program. One can think of this as a "compliance inspection" of the OIGs. To the extent that the OIGs followed the procedures established for them, and to the extent that the procedures were well designed to enhance accountability and performance, this "compliance inspection" can tell us whether the institutions are succeeding. The primary data we have accumulated for performing this task are the materials we have already presented on the strategies being pursued by the IGs, the annual reports of the IGs, and some data published by the PCIE.

A harder task is to look at what can be seen of the impact of the OIGs on government's accountability and performance. One can think of this as a "performance inspection" of the OIGs. In observing the impact of the OIGs, it is necessary to become more precise about what is meant by "accountability" and "performance." As we have seen, there are some troubling ambiguities in these concepts. "Accountability" seems to be a procedural virtue associated with the collection and publication of accurate data about program performance.[142] But whether this is true or not often depends on the specific terms of accountability. The issue, then, is exactly what the OIGs are responsible for producing.

One concept is that the OIGs are responsible for "enhanced financial integrity." This, in turn, might be reflected in "improved detection of fraud and abuse," "increased recoveries of losses associated with fraud and abuse," or "improved procedures for preventing fraud and abuse."

A second concept is that the OIGs are responsible for "reduced costs for given levels of services." One might assume that this is the same as "enhanced financial integrity" since success in this domain will mean fewer losses to fraud and abuse, and therefore lower costs. The catch, however, is that money must often be spent to enhance financial integrity. The OIGs themselves, for example, represent a cost that must be paid. In addition, their recommendations may often require greater levels of effort and care by program staff. That, too, will cost money. Finally, the quality of the service to clients may be adversely affected. It may become slower, more intrusive, or less tailored to their individual requirements than would be true in a world in which the procedures were less exacting. Of course, one may judge reductions in these dimensions of service to the program's clients as insignificant in value compared with improved representations of financial integrity that can now be made to the taxpayers and their representatives who are also "customers" of the government's program. But the point is that the pursuit of financial integrity will change the performance characteristics of the program and therefore change its value to both clients and the broader public that provides the resources for the programs. In principle, then, the pursuit of financial integrity might increase rather than reduce the costs of the program per unit of service delivered to clients and the broader public.

A third concept is that the OIGs are responsible for "enhanced efficiency and effectiveness." This concept is very closely related to "reduced costs per unit of service." Indeed, if we hold the definition of a unit of service constant, and if we evaluate a program at a single moment in time, then the concepts are identical. But what the idea of improved efficiency emphasizes in addition to reduced costs is the importance of (1) defining the elements of the program's operation that have value to clients and the broader public (for example, the speed, nonintrusiveness, and tailored quality of the program as well as its financial integrity and overall cost); (2) balancing these competing aspects of the program or service in a politically responsible way; and (3) recognizing that the balance in these values, as well as the procedures and technologies for delivering the services, will change over time. In short, the concept of overall efficiency tries to keep all the costs of program operations in view, see them in relationship to different valued attributes of the program, and place them in a dynamic context in which both program procedures and values can change. In this conception, financial integrity might be enhanced, but only at the expense of reduced performance in some attributes of the service and perhaps a reduced capacity to innovate in the future.

In conducting a "performance inspection" of the OIGs against any of these objectives, we have essentially two data sources on which to rely. The most important are cases describing the engagement of the Inspectors-General in the operations of two departments and two programs in each department.[143] These cases include a department with long experience with IGs and one with little experience. The programs include those directly administered by the federal government and those indirectly administered; those that involve individual clients and those that involve larger organizations as clients; those that involve loans and those that involve direct payments; and those that involve middle-class or wealthy people and those that involve poor people. The task in examining these cases is to discern how the IGs have shaped their operations. The second data source is discussion and comments from the program managers who met with us and the IGs in open-ended meetings.[144]

Finally, in trying to determine the ultimate value of the IGs, we might go beyond the "performance audit" and try to determine exactly how much of the changes in government performance we observe can be attributed directly to the IGs. This might seem to be a trivial problem. All we need to do is examine the performance of government programs before and after scrutiny by the OIG. This would allow us to examine the "specific deterrent effects" of OIGs on program operations. Alternatively, we could examine OIG proposals for policy changes, determine how many of them were adopted, and examine how the performance of the programs changed in relevant dimensions.

Unfortunately, these methods cannot rule out other explanations for changes observed in program performance. Many programs may have moved in the same directions as direct OIG scrutiny would move them by the prospect or reality of congressional investigation, press scrutiny, the demands of top management in the departments, or even the threat of IG action. In such a world, direct IG scrutiny might influence program operations very little. Similarly, many specific proposals made by OIGs for program improvements have been made before—sometimes even by program managers. Again, the separate and partial contribution of the OIGs might be impossible to disentangle. Since our data are limited, and this problem difficult to handle even with large quantities of data, we will make no effort to distinguish the effects of the OIGs alone from broader forces. Instead, throughout, we will entertain the idea that the most important impact of the OIGs is to provide a rallying point for those who want to increase the financial integrity and efficiency of government.

A Compliance Inspection of the Offices of Inspectors-General

As we have seen, the OIGs have positioned themselves comfortably within the broad mandate created by Congress and the PCIE. Inevitably, the bulk of their activities remain in the traditional areas of investigation and audit. That is what Congress seems to have intended. It is also consistent with the current capacities of the OIGs. The OIGs have not benefited from any large increase in resources. They have held steady at a time when much of the government is shrinking, so it is quite possible that their share of government expenditures has increased. But if they were to improve their performance in these traditional areas, it would have to come from more efficient or effective use of the resources available to them.

In the pursuit of enhanced efficiency and effectiveness in the performance of these traditional functions, the OIGs have shown imagination and determination. With respect to investigations, they have widened the use of hot lines to receive tips and complaints about incidents of fraud or abuse,[145] developed and used innovative investigative techniques (such as computer matching and undercover operations),[146] and established appropriate relations with prosecuting organizations (specifically, with the FBI and the Criminal Division of the Department of Justice).[147] There are still some tensions in the best way to bring investigations to a close and to use them in the context of audits. For example, some agencies prefer that their own investigators handle investigations and resolve the matter through administrative actions by the organization, while others prefer to pursue formal prosecutions which brings them into complex relations with the FBI and U.S. Attorneys. Similarly, the pursuit of formal criminal investigations often slows down audits and administrative actions against employees because the secrecy and legal requirements that govern the process of criminal investigation preempt less formal, broader, and faster administrative efforts to gather information. For example, the implementation of audit recommendations in the FECA Program was delayed while the investigations unit wrapped up a fraud investigation.[148] But generally speaking, the level, quality, and focus of investigative activities have all improved since the formation of the OIGs.

With respect to audits, there have been similar improvements. One key change has been the decision to delegate audit responsibility to others to close the "audit gap."[149] A second has been improved targeting of programs that seem most "vulnerable"—an effort that has been aided by OMB's mandate to program managers to do "vulnerability assessments" of their programs, as well as the initiation of some analytic planning capabilities within the OIGs. A third has been experiments with the use of personal computers to improve the efficiency of audits. The OIGs seem to be squeezing a few more audits out of a fixed capacity.

While the bulk of the OIGs' activities remain in these traditional areas, the fastest growing component of their function lies in the area of *prevention* of fraud, waste, and abuse. This capacity has developed in two ways. First, both investigators and auditors in the normal course of their duties to *detect* fraud, waste, and abuse have kept thinking independently about ways to prevent these problems in the future. For example, in DOL a fraud investigation resulted in recommendations for improved control over access to government computers and improved documentation and review of payments authorized.[150] Similarly, in FmHA, an audit of some large Business and Industrial Loans led to the development of tighter procedures governing outside contacts between high program officials and clients.[151] Second, the central thrust of OIG activity has shifted in the direction of emphasizing preventive activities. Indeed, what can be seen across all the OIGs (with the encouragement and acceptance of both Congress and the PCIE) is a gradual evolution away from investigations toward audits, and increased experimentation with more flexible methods called "inspections."[152] This naturally carries them from fraud to waste and abuse and from detection to the design of administrative systems to prevent all kinds of fraud, waste, and abuse.

It is also significant that the PCIE and Congress are beginning to see that the financial returns to the government of detecting and recovering fraud, waste, and abuse seem trivial compared with the potential returns from prevention. Indeed, in accounting for the "total monetary impact" of the OIGs (understood as savings to the federal government resulting from OIG activity), recoveries from past instances of corruption account for less than 5 percent of the estimated impact.[153] This tends to push the OIGs even further and faster in the direction of *preventing* fraud, waste, and abuse.

As the OIGs move toward focusing their efforts on preventing fraud, waste, and abuse, the goal of promoting efficiency also assumes more importance, but their commitment to this task remains diffuse and ambivalent. When they can make the idea of promoting efficiency identical to the idea of enhanced financial integrity and improved accountability, they are, of course, quite interested in the idea. Moreover, their current interest in "inspections" suggests a growing interest in promoting efficiency in a broader sense—one that is concerned with outputs as well as procedures and with innovation as well as compliance with rules.[154] But the broadest idea of promoting efficiency is, in practice, regarded still as an ideal to aspire to rather than the central task of an organization of investigators and auditors.

It is interesting to note that in these areas the IGs themselves are generally more forward thinking than their organizations. The IGs are more interested than their deputies or troops in the prevention of fraud, waste, and abuse than in detection and in the promotion of efficiency than in prevention. That is as it should be, for the IGs must represent the future of their organizations rather than their past and must challenge their investigators and auditors to perform in unfamiliar areas. Moreover, the IGs are in the best position to see the patterns emerging from their investigations and audits and to see how these patterns might be accommodated within the operations of the organization as a whole.

A Performance Inspection of the Offices of Inspectors-General

The most immediate consequences of the creation of the Offices of Inspectors-General can be seen in the increased detection of fraud, waste, and abuse; in increased prosecutions and financial recoveries from those who have committed fraud; and in increased rates of audit resolutions and financial recoveries from those agencies that have used government money abusively or wastefully.

ENHANCED FINANCIAL INTEGRITY: THE IMPROVED DETECTION OF FRAUD AND ABUSE

According to the PCIE, allegations of fraud, waste, and abuse reported to OIGs have increased from about 10,000 per year in FY 1981 to more than 25,000 in FY 1983.[155] Successful prosecutions have increased from a little more than 1,000 in FY 1981 to a little less than 4,000 in FY 1983.[156] Actions against government employees and contractors have increased from 700 in FY 1981 to 2,500 in FY 1983.[157] While there is some uncertainty about the accuracy of these numbers, they do suggest heightened levels of investigative and audit activity.

The effect of OIGs on audit activity, resolution, and debt collection is illustrated best by the Department of Labor and its CETA Program.[158] In 1973 the Comprehensive Employment and Training Act was enacted to place a myriad of federally sponsored employment and training programs under the control of local agencies designated as "prime sponsors" of the federal employment program. There were about 475 "prime sponsors" and over 55,000 subcontractors.[159] Supported programs included those such as Job Corps directed at "structural" employment problems and Public Service Employment directed at "cyclical" employment problems. By 1978 the cyclical aspect of the program had grown rapidly, and there was widespread congressional concern about the integrity of the program. As a result, Congress enacted legislation to tighten up the program and improve its management. Even with these reforms, however, the DOL Inspectors-General found a great deal of work to do.

The most embarrassing problem was an audit gap that left most "prime sponsors" unexamined throughout the 1970s. OIG responded by making CETA its first priority. Perhaps even more important, it proposed a regulation that would require prime sponsors to secure their own audits. This immediately increased the total number of audits. While the first round of audits revealed many problems, the second round in 1982 produced more satisfactory results.[160] Apparently the audit process is a necessary part of both developing and teaching policies governing appropriate expenditures in new programs.

The increase in the number of audits in DOL meant that a backlog of unresolved audits also grew. An audit is "resolved" when regional management, the auditors, and the local prime sponsor agree that the audit report is final. This report can be appealed to an administrative law judge in DOL and further negotiations can occur at that stage. But the first step is to produce an audit resolution. That enterprise, too, languished due to managerial neglect. In 1978 the objective of reducing audit backlogs by 10 percent per year was added to the performance standards of DOL regional managers, and the backlog began to shrink.[161] The arrival of the OIG accelerated the action, however. New procedures for resolving audits were written in consultation with local prime sponsors and DOL regional managers. The wide consultation was designed to raise the issue on managers' agendas, to inform them about the procedures, and to resolve particular policy issues that were delaying audit resolutions.[162] New agreements were made about troublesome cost items such as time and attendance records for Public Sector Employment workers, meal costs at administrative meetings, line-item overexpenditures, and so on.[163] These measures served to reduce the resolution backlog. Still, by January 1981, at the start of the Reagan Administration, almost 800 unresolved audits in DOL, accounting for more than $303 million in questioned costs, remained.[164]

These unresolved cases represented an obvious management target not only to the OIGs, but also to the incoming Assistant Secretary for Employment and Training, Albert Angrisani. He established an objective of "zero backlog" by the end of the fiscal year (September 1981).[165] The OIG assisted his efforts in two ways: by lending the technical and moral support of the office to this effort (indeed, part of this support involved *withdrawing* some nit-picking objections in the interest of moving toward an audit resolution)[166] and by assisting in the development of an automated system that turned up unresolved audits, or audits that were being resolved in terms too favorable to the local prime sponsors, and making them quite visible throughout the department.[167] Together, and against the background of strong congressional and PCIE support, Angrisani achieved his objective.

This success set the stage for increased pressure for debt collecting. The resolution of an audit left the prime sponsor with a debt to be paid to DOL. Traditionally, collection of the debts has been neglected in the department. The debts could be appealed to an administrative law judge for final resolution, and often were if the amounts were large and the audit resolution process had been cantankerous. The debts did not have to be paid, nor was any interest charged, while the issue was under appeal. In addition, the debts could be settled by devices other than direct cash payments. The local agency could agree to provide additional services at no cost to the government or to accept a reduction in next year's grant. Finally, since DOL regional managers needed the prime sponsors to achieve their performance objectives, there was little incentive to antagonize them about past debts when the current problem was performance. For all these reasons, debt collection went as slowly as audits and audit resolutions.[168]

These procedures changed dramatically under Angrisani's leadership. He could not prevent the agencies from appealing decisions, but he changed the regulations so that agencies would be charged interest on their debts while their cases were being appealed.[169] He also made it clear that most debts should be settled in cash.[170] Finally, as in the case of audit resolutions, he made DOL regional managers personally responsible for debt collections and forbade any compromises on debts to be repaid for fraudulent activities. Exactly how much cash has actually been reclaimed as a result of this initiative remains unclear. What has appeared, however, is mounting political pressure on the Department of Labor from clients groups to establish a tolerable rate of "errors" in CETA expenditures.[171]

While this history of increasing audit capacity in CETA programs is impressive, it is valuable to keep it in perspective. For the four years from 1978 to 1982 IG audits disallowed, on average, 2.5 percent of the audited expenditures. The proportion of these questioned costs that has been finally disallowed has averaged between 30 and 15 percent. So, about 1 percent of the total costs for CETA have been finally disallowed.[172]

The numbers from the PCIE and the evidence from DOL suggest that there have been significant increases in the detection of fraud, waste, and abuse through investigation and audit. To the extent that the detection of fraud, waste, and abuse indicates more "accountability" in the system, this performance means that the IGs, and the managers with whom they have worked, have enhanced accountability. Moreover, to the extent that financial recoveries and the deterrence of future fraud, waste, and abuse resulted from these efforts, the OIGs have "reduced fraud, waste, and abuse" and "enhanced financial integrity." We cannot be certain of this. Nor can we be certain that it was the OIGs rather than some broader trends that produced these effects. But if we had to bet, we would bet that these effects had been produced.

REDUCED COSTS AND THE PROMOTION OF EFFICIENCY

A harder question to answer is whether the OIGs have reduced the costs of government or increased efficiency. The reason is that we must be able to evaluate what happened to total costs of government and the value of government output as well as reductions in fraud, waste, and abuse. To those who value accountability and financial integrity *intrinsically* as features of government programs, the OIGs clearly increased the value of government programs. But to those who value these things only as devices for increasing the overall *efficiency* of government, the answer is less clear. The reason is that it is possible that the OIGs increased overall cost and reduced government output at the same time that they were increasing accountability and enhancing financial integrity.

Part of the problem in measuring gains in "efficiency" and the value of government programs is that there are different "consumers" of government services. To some, the important consumers of government services are the taxpayers and voters. After all, it is their money and their tolerance of government involvement that provide the basic resources for programs to continue. Moreover, it is their satisfaction with the programs as well as the benefits to clients that constitute the overall public value of the program. When we are thinking about these consumers, it is quite natural to look at a program in terms of its "integrity"; that is, its ability to deliver promised benefits (and obligations) according to policies and procedures agreed to in advance. To others, the consumers of government services are the clients of government programs. When we are concentrating on the clients, it is natural to think of government production as increasing when the quantity and quality of services to the clients increase—that is, when more of those eligible for a program receive its benefits, when the process of determining eligibility becomes quicker and less intrusive, when benefits can be tailored more precisely to individual needs and opportunities, and so on.

There is a tendency to think of the interests of these different customers as being opposed. The overseeing, authorizing public prefers stricter standards, more accurate eligibility determination, and tight control over individual officials. The clients of programs prefer greater openness, faster and less intrusive decisions, and more discretion for officials. To this degree, the groups are opposed. Probably everyone in the society, however, would value the different attributes of the program in the same way: other things being equal, everyone would prefer faster, less intrusive, and more accurate eligibility determination; lower administrative costs per unit of service; greater financial integrity and accountability; and so on. Where people differ is on the relative importance they attach to these attributes of performance. It is tempting to value speed and nonintrusiveness at the expense of accuracy when we are giving out driver's licenses or emergency loans to businesses and to reverse the emphasis when we are delivering food stamps or unemployment compensation. It is the task of politics to balance the interests of the different consuming groups in the policies that guide the program and the task of administration to produce as much of all of these desired qualities as possible.

The IGs enter this discussion at the point where they make proposals designed to change the procedures of programs in ways that will make them less vulnerable to fraud, waste, and abuse (their prevention function) or where they have some ideas about how to promote overall efficiency (their efficiency function). The proposed changes in administrative procedures will often change the costs, quantity, and quality of the government program as delivered to both clients and overseers. If it is a "good" proposal, some important attributes of a program (such as its financial integrity) will improve without costing much in terms of administrative costs or degraded service. If it is a "bad" proposal, the implementation of the proposed policies may cost more or degrade performance more than it increases the overall accountability of the program. Judging whether a proposed change is good or bad is partly a technical-empirical issue. That is, one must judge how the incorporation of the proposed procedure will affect the different aspects of program performance. But it is also a political-normative issue, for one must judge how much value is produced to overseers and clients by incorporating the proposed change and whose interests matter more.

The PCIE clearly understands the potential importance of IG prevention and efficiency-promoting functions. In its early reports, it referred to savings generated by "cost avoidances."[173] In its most recent report, it claims $26.7 billion in "commitments from agency managers to more efficiently use resources" since 1981.[174] Leaving aside the question of whether these numbers are accurate, and how many of these commitments will actually be implemented and produce the imagined results, there is a conceptual problem with these numbers. They do not address the issue of what has happened to the value of the output of various programs. There is an implied assumption that government production remains constant, or if it changes it comes closer to the way in which everyone intended the program to operate all along. Thus, for example, if the FECA Program begins relying more extensively on rehabilitation rather than payments, and if the FmHA Emergency Loan Program restricts its loans to cover direct losses and eliminates loans to cover the costs of people moving to new businesses in the face of natural disasters, then the society avoids some costs. But the society has not altered the output of the program or has altered it only in ways that more precisely realize the purposes of the program. Of course, to the extent that Congress and political executives assent to such changes, we may reasonably say that a new and proper balance has been struck among the desired features of a program's performance. But there is an important distortion in the PCIE reports that comes from its silence on the question of what has happened to the quantity and quality of government production as costs are being "avoided" or managers are making commitments to "greater efficiency."

One way to get a handle on what is going on behind these figures is to examine the sorts of changes that Inspectors-General succeed in making in program operations. Appendix B lists all the different changes in program operations observed in our case studies of OIGs in federal departments. As we review the items listed in Appendix B, we see many things that are clearly desirable. But it is also clear that the emphasis of most changes are on "cost avoidances" or "minimizing the financial exposure of government" to its clients. As long as we don't think about product, "costs avoided" sounds find. But once we begin thinking of the value of service to clients as well as overseers (and understand that many overseers also want service to clients), the virtues of cost avoidance seem less clear. After all, the service that government is delivering to clients in many of these programs is *financial assistance*. Thus, in order to deliver more service, a program must increase its "financial exposure." The resolution of this apparent conflict lies in the idea of maintaining program integrity. The task of the program is to deliver financial assistance to those intended to receive it. Often this involves redefining both the program and the product, as well as controlling costs within a given program. At that point, everyone may prefer the new program to the old, but what has changed is the character of the product as well as the cost of producing the product.

It is important to understand that the interests of client and overseer are not always opposed. In the Food Stamp Program, for example, the desire to reduce food stamp trafficking and diversion among overseers turned out to be consistent with the interests of food stamp clients in one aspect of the program—"block purchase requirements,"[175] which required clients of the Food Stamp Program to purchase a large minimum quantity of stamps.

This was originally designed to reduce administrative costs in the program by minimizing the number of transactions. It had the effect of preventing many clients from being able to purchase food stamps (because they could not make the required minimum level of purchase), and it made the system vulnerable to fraud (since large numbers of food stamps were being held by clients who could distribute them to others—many of whom were ineligible). Since nobody liked this feature of the program, it was eliminated. This challenged the program's managers to create a faster, more exact method of issuing "authorization to purchase" to clients and, in the end, may have increased overall administrative costs.[176] But the decision to eliminate block purchase requirements allowed better service to clients and reduced vulnerability to fraud. Similarly, in the FECA Program it is possible that both overseers and clients of the program benefited from pressures created by the OIG to use more rehabilitation programs at an earlier stage to return federal workers to employability in their organizations.[177] This policy was in the interest of the overseers because it limited governmental financial exposure. It was in the interest of the clients because it reduced their financial dependency.

It is also important to understand that OIG interests in minimizing governmental financial exposure affect rich and powerful clients of government as well as poor. The OIGs played a major role in keeping politically and economically powerful corporations from misusing the loan programs of the FmHA for their purposes.[178] They also put pressure on food stamp wholesalers to pay their bills to the federal government more quickly so that the government could earn the interest on the money rather than the wholesalers.[179] Finally, in the FECA Program, IG proposals reduced fraud by physicians and medical providers as well as by clients.[180]

SUMMARY

Thus, in gauging the impact of OIGs on government operations, we can posit the following. First, OIGs seem to be detecting more fraud, waste, and abuse and moving more aggressively to recover losses than their predecessor units did. To the extent that these actions represent gains in accountability and financial integrity, we may say that they have contributed to these objectives.

Second, increasingly OIGs see their major opportunities to contribute to government performance in terms of proposed administrative changes that would *prevent* fraud, waste, and abuse. To the extent that the deterrence resulting from improved detection and more aggressive efforts to prosecute and recover losses reduces fraud, waste, and abuse, and to the extent that their proposals to make administrative procedures less vulnerable are adopted and prove to be effective, the OIGs will also be making a major contribution to one notion of accountability and financial integrity.

Third, the OIGs, contributions to enhanced financial integrity are not necessarily the same as improved efficiency. Efficiency has to do with the value of government output to clients as well as overseers, and to overseers who balance the interests in financial integrity and service to clients in different ways. These interests are not always in conflict, and OIGs have done excellent work in finding situations in which both interests can be advanced. But when these interests are in conflict, political-normative judgments must be made about the goals and values of the programs. The OIGs often contribute to that discussion by revealing questionable actions by program officials and forcing a debate among congressional overseers, program managers, and those representing clients to determine how the balance should be struck. To the extent that these discussions lead to new policies enacted in legislation, administrative rulings, or agency practices that balance the competing interests more precisely, we may say that efficiency has increased as well. The best examples of such negotiations have occurred in the Food Stamp Program, the CETA Program, and the FmHA Business and Industrial Loan Program.[181]

The OIGs seem to face two great risks in influencing government operations. One risk is that they, their interests in promoting financial integrity, and their proposals will not be taken seriously enough by program managers. Lest one think this unlikely, it is sufficient to point out that all of the cases we studied revealed consistent failures of management to respond to OIG recommendations, which consequently led to problems.[182] A second great risk is that the OIGs will be taken too seriously. After all, as we have seen, the pursuit of financial integrity by itself is not necessarily identical to the concept of enhanced accountability, nor to increased efficiency. If the "principals" in Congress, the executive branch, and the courts want products of a certain type and are willing to spend only limited amounts for computers and administrative costs, they may accept some losses in financial integrity without feeling that their "agent" has been unaccountable. The agent may have produced exactly what the principals wanted.

Perhaps the OIGs' greatest opportunity to contribute to government operations is to force a conversation among the principals on the *terms* of accountability. Their success in this role depends on the way that they manage their engagement with political overseers in Congress, the press, and elsewhere, and with program managers who must carry out or adjust their proposals. Thus, in evaluating the ultimate impact of the Inspectors-General, it is important that we examine briefly the character of this encounter with the political environment and the program managers in establishing the terms of accountability.

Relations with Program Management and Political Oversight

The managers of programs—both political executives and career managers—are crucially important to the success of the OIGs. Without management's cooperation, IG proposals for the prevention of fraud, waste, and abuse or for improved efficiency would be stillborn. Similarly, without management's knowledge of program operations, the character of the clients, and its political history, OIG assumptions about improved efficiency may be badly mistaken. And without management's cooperation in investigations and audits, it would be difficult for the IGs to perform their jobs well. It is these simple facts that impel IGs toward managers and encourage them to want to join the "management team."

At the same time, it is important for IGs to maintain distance from the managers. This is true partly because they have the responsibility for developing objective facts about program operations. If they get "too close" to management, they may be tempted to conceal facts that create problems for managers. Distance is also important, however, because the IGs stand for a slightly different mix of values than program managers. Their notion of accountability would emphasize financial integrity and compliance with the literal terms of policies and programs over vaguer notions of efficiency and performance in the spirit of a principal's aspirations. Program managers generally stand for the broader and fuzzier notion—though there are program managers who huddle in the shelter of clear policies and procedures and IGs who are willing to eliminate some useless red tape in the interests of improved program performance. Distance is also important to the IGs because it may allow them to see something in a program that the manager was unable to see. So, the IGs need to cultivate distance from as well as obligations to and responsibility for program management.

The OIGs have an equally awkward relationship with the political sphere of Congress and the press. The offices were created as an instrument of congressional oversight, and as a result have important formal and informal ties to Congress. In addition, because fraud, waste, and abuse always makes good copy for the media, the IGs find that they have convenient formal and informal access to the press. These relationships to the political world are important to the IGs because they provide a platform from which to press their proposals on management. If management is unresponsive, the IGs can always go to Congress or the press. Indeed, this threat is implicit in much of their negotiations with management. Political support and the values they stand for allow IGs to gain a hearing from management that might otherwise be absent.

At the same time, the relationships to political oversight create difficulties for the IGs. Generally speaking, program managers prefer that their problems be handled in less visible administrative proceedings than in Congress and the press, because (1) they resent the damage to their public reputation; (2) they dislike the loss of credibility and autonomy that attends political interventions; and (3) they find it becomes increasingly difficult to work out a reasoned compromise regarding the organization and operations of their programs when the issues are being debated among an indignant, outraged public whose attention is focused on some features of the program's performance. When an IG deliberately or unwittingly escalates an issue, then, the program managers are likely to respond with anger and indignation. They will fight the IGs rather than try to solve the problem. This conflict does neither the IGs nor the program managers nor the performance of the program much good. This is the opposite side of the coin of the IG's power: when used implicitly for influence, it is helpful; when used explicitly, new problems and difficulties appear.

A second problem resulting from close connections to political oversight is that the IGs sometimes end up focusing their efforts on areas that become politically hot rather than substantively important. Of course, the two are often related. But the correlation is not perfect. And, as the IGs struggle to establish that they are on top of an agency's problems, they may well gravitate toward issues that are politically salient rather than substantively significant. Indeed, it is surprising how often IG actions in our cases were occurring simultaneously with extensive press coverage and with congressional action. The relationship is particularly clear in the case of the press involvement in the FmHA Emergency Loan and Business and Industrial Loan Programs[183] and congressional involvement in medical provider fraud in the FECA Program.[184] Whether the IG got involved because of political attention, whether his involvement caused political attention, or whether both were provoked by an important substantive problem within the program could be debated forever. The timing of events never quite provides an answer because there is usually an intertwining history of IG, press, and congressional interest in programs that sometimes escalates into flare-ups, and sometimes not. At any rate, the question of exactly how IGs should respond to and use political interest in fraud, waste, and abuse in managing their relationships with line management is a key issue because it largely determines their success in improving efficiency.

While the lessons to be learned from our cases and interviews about how to manage these relationships are not entirely clear, the following principles seem to be a useful starting point. First, it seems clear that IGs need access to the political environment to be able to press their concerns on program managers. Our cases are full of instances in which IG suggestions were made, but went unheeded by management. This is particularly well documented in the case of FECA. The IG's proposals to prevent fraud by FECA employees were ignored, and when he followed his proposals with an audit, it revealed actual instances of fraud of exactly the type that would have been prevented by the security measures he proposed.[185]

Second, it also seems clear that the effectiveness of IGs is greatest when they can operate with the implicit threat of publicity and congressional attention rather than its reality. When an issue escalates, there is a real risk that program managers will dig in their heels, frustrating implementation of proposed changes. There is also the risk that the issues surrounding the operations of a program will be discussed too much in the IG's terms, and the important contributions that managers could make to balancing interests in financial integrity, low-cost administration, and overall efficiency will be eliminated from the debate. In short, technical creativity as well as judiciousness in balancing the social values produced through the operations of the program may be driven out by intense but short-lived political debate. This is perhaps most obvious in the congressional response to fraud, waste, and abuse in HEW.[186]

Third, the impact of the IGs may be greatest when they allow management to assume much of the initiative for solving their agencies' problems and much of the credit for doing so. In a particularly powerful incident in our cases, FECA managers happily accepted some IG proposals once the IG indicated (falsely) that management had initiated the IG investigation.[187] This suggests how great a stake management has in defending its overall responsibility for a program. It almost seems that it is as important for managers to remain in the saddle as it is for them to direct their programs toward particular visions. If true, this means that there should be wide latitude for the IGs to be successful, as long as they share the credit. Sharing credit should not be hard for the IGs since many of their ideas are not particularly novel. But desirable as it is to share credit, the IGs are under pressure from Congress and the PCIE to produce on their own, which sometimes leads them to exaggerate the magnitude of their contribution.

Fourth, the impact of the IGs is probably the greatest when the political environment shifts in their direction. The incoming Reagan Administration carried a general mandate to enhance the financial integrity of government programs. This meant not only that the IGs became much more important and prominent, but also that they were joined by aggressive program managers interested in the same goals. This was most clear in the case of Angrisani at the Department of Labor.[188] When the IGs and political executives share objectives, and budget pressures are at work, it is almost inevitable that IG proposals will be accepted.

Fifth, the impact of the IGs seems to be growing as a function of experience. This effect is hard to distinguish from the effects of a shift in political values. But as was evident from our meetings with the IGs and program managers, it seems that IGs and managers are learning to work together. Some of the tension is disappearing from their relationship as they become familiar with one another and more tolerant of the values each represents.

Finally, the IGs seem to be the most valuable when they can convene and sustain a conversation among all those who have a role in creating the conditions under which fraud, waste, and abuse can occur. Typically, this includes Congress and local managers of programs, as well as federal managers. Indeed, in many situations, federal managers are the most obvious but the least useful target. The problems sometimes lie in the design of the program or in the complex networks of local administration. In organizing this discussion, however, it is crucial for the participants to keep their eyes on the *product* and *efficiency*, as well as cost and financial integrity. Otherwise, the government may become "accountable" in some narrow sense, but actually lose "accountability" in a broader sense which involves the quantity and quality of government programs as viewed by both overseers and clients.

Part V Summary and Conclusions

The central issue posed by this preliminary assessment of the Offices of Inspectors-General is whether they are increasing the accountability of the government and improving its performance or not. Behind this apparently straightforward question lie some problematic issues which make assessment difficult.

Perhaps the most important issue is that some tension exists between the ideas of improved accountability and improved performance. Accountability has to do with the capacity of an agent to satisfy a principal that resources entrusted to him for specific purposes are being used well.[189] Performance has to do with the ability of the agent to produce things of value to the principal at the lowest possible cost in terms of resources utilized. In general, accountability is achieved by showing the principal that resources are being used according to the terms set out in the original agreement—in the public sector, by showing that resources are being used according to preannounced policies and procedures. This is consistent with the idea of performance if the policies and procedures represent an efficient way of producing the result the principal intended.

Accountability differs from performance, however, in situations in which staying within existing policies and procedures results in lower production of things desired by the principals than could be achieved if the procedures were adjusted or relaxed. Accountability may also differ from performance in that accountability consumes resources that could, in principle, be used for production. As the demand for accountability grows, administrative costs will rise and managerial attention will be diverted. If these demands stimulate improvements in a slovenly, inefficient system or inspire management to work harder, then the costs of increased accountability may be offset by improvements in performance that were discovered through the improved machinery of accountability, or simply through motivational effects. On the other hand, if the system is already performing well, increased demands for accountability will impose costs without any benefits in terms of enhanced quantity or quality of performance.

Tension also exists between the ideas of "enhanced financial integrity" or "reduced fraud, waste, and abuse," on the one hand, and the "promotion of economy and efficiency," on the other. It is obvious that if clients or employees of the government are stealing money or using it for inappropriate purposes, then some potential value in government services is being lost: money is being consumed without any (or as much) of what the government intended to produce being produced. It is also obvious that the frequency of such events could be reduced by increasing administrative measures to detect such events once they have occurred, and by designing procedures that would prevent them from happening by making it much more likely that the events would be observed either in the short or long run.

What is not obvious is that the use of these measures to reduce fraud, waste, and abuse would necessarily increase efficiency and effectiveness. On the positive side, they would clearly reduce instances of wasted money and therefore increase the amount of money available for proper purposes. In addition, since some of the most important consumers of government programs—namely, the congressmen and voters who support the programs with their tax dollars—tend to value the financial integrity of the program as an important attribute of the program independently of its other characteristics (such as total cost and quantity and quality of services to clients), the efforts to reduce fraud, waste, and abuse will increase the value of the programs to some "consumers" of government services.

On the negative side, detection of past instances of fraud, waste, and abuse comes only at a price. People must be paid to examine records. They must also be paid to perform investigations that check the validity of the records. These costs are accrued as part of the administrative costs of the program.

In addition, the new administrative procedures designed to control fraud, waste, and abuse by *creating* new records, or new points in the system where an action must be reviewed by someone else, also carry a price. Part of the price comes in the form of increased resources applied by the agency to the completion of a given transaction. If two new forms must be completed, and each must be checked by a supervisor, the "technology" for producing a given transaction has become more expensive.

Another part of the price, however, comes in the form of reduced quantities and qualities of service to individual clients. Clients are not the only consumers of government services; as noted above, the general public and its representatives must be viewed as consumers as well. But the satisfaction of clients with the government service is of some importance to the overall efficiency, effectiveness, and value of government services. From the clients' point of view, if the procedures become slower, or more intrusive, or less capable of responding to specific aspects of their individual situation, or if many of the costs of establishing their eligibility are shifted to them, then the service is less attractive: less value for them is being produced. Such things might be easy to ignore if we are thinking about welfare clients or disabled federal employees, but they are much more apparent if we think about issuing driver's licenses, making emergency loans to farmers who are victims of natural disasters, or conducting tax audits. Being concerned about the service aspects in programs involving the rich and middle class means that we should be aware of them in programs involving the poor as well. To the extent that these attributes of service to clients have value, it is possible that they will be adversely affected by the administrative procedures designed to reduce fraud, waste, and abuse.

The point of drawing this distinction is not to argue that efforts to control fraud, waste, and abuse will always reduce government efficiency. They might or they might not. The point is to establish the distinction between controlling one aspect of cost and the overall concepts of efficiency, effectiveness, and value. It would never occur to a manager of a retail bookstore to install procedures to control shoplifting without considering how much it would cost, how big an effect it would have on levels of theft, whether the methods would affect the overall attractiveness of his store, and how his tolerance of continued shoplifting might look to his lenders and partners. And it shouldn't occur to government managers to install measures against fraud, waste, and abuse until they have looked at these aspect of the proposed methods and their current situation. In essence, then, the task is to avoid the trap of equating cost control with efficiency and to see that what accountability in the public sector should mean is efficient performance to both clients and overseers of the programs.

In addition to difficulties attributable to subtle conceptual issues lying behind apparently simple concepts, our investigation was hampered by the difficulty of distinguishing the separate effects of the OIGs from all the other factors operating on government managers and programs. After all, the manager's responsibilities include many of the responsibilities of the OIGs; he might therefore have taken unilateral action in the direction of OIG recommendations even if the OIG had not made them. Indeed, in the cases we reviewed, many OIG proposals had previously been made by management. Similarly, many other institutions of accountability surround managers. In some of our cases, offices of administration and management developed reforms and created pressures on program managers that were similar to those created by the OIGs. In others, congressional committees performed the same function. And perhaps the most significant factor shaping both OIG conduct and the response of program managers was the electoral mandate of Ronald Reagan, which moved the entire government in the direction of values the OIGs represented.

Conclusions About the Impact of the Offices of Inspectors-General

For the reasons discussed above, it is hard to come to a definitive answer as to whether the OIGs have increased or decreased the accountability and performance of government. In presenting our conclusions it is useful to return to three alternative hypotheses formulated at the outset of our inquiry.

Hypothesis I is that the OIGs would enhance both the accountability and performance of government programs. The arguments that made this hypothesis plausible are essentially those that persuaded Congress to pass the IG statute: that the vast expansion of government programs (and the corresponding emphasis on government output) had left the programs vulnerable to fraud and corruption and that the government's efforts to deal with this problem were too small, badly organized, and without influence. Since the OIGs represented a solution to these problems, the establishment of the OIGs would strengthen the accountability of the government.

Hypothesis II is that the OIGs would have little independent effect on the performance of government. The theory that supported this hypothesis is essentially that of the natural evolution of politics and administration. Just as the economic prosperity of the 1960s stimulated a spirit of generosity verging on license, the economic hardships of the late 1970s fostered a sense of fiscal responsibility tending toward niggardliness. This shift in mood would inevitably be reflected in the administration of government programs. Accountants and hard-nosed managers would replace social workers and "bleeding hearts" at the head of government programs. Sensing the change in values that emphasized overseers over clients and accountability over performance, employees throughout the system would use their discretion to err on the side of caution rather than responsiveness in delivering services. The results would be indistinguishable from what would have occurred had the OIGs become influential, but they would not be the cause.

Hypothesis III is the most radical: the OIGs might increase accountability, but only at the cost of *reducing* the overall efficiency and effectiveness of government. Three observations made this hypothesis plausible. First, it is important to see the analytic distinction between the concepts of accountability, fiscal integrity, and the control of fraud, waste, and abuse, on the one hand, and the concepts of efficiency and effectiveness, on the other, to avoid the erroneous assumption that improvements in one area are the same as improvements in the other. Second, it is important to understand that the determination of the OIGs to be objective in defining fraud, waste, and abuse, and to be successful in controlling it, would lead to the creation of very narrow rules controlling government expenditures and multiple levels of review to check compliance with the rules. This could reduce efficiency and effectiveness by discouraging innovation, demoralizing managers, and tangling government programs in additional red tape. Third, since other systems of accountability already existed, it is possible that government managers had already incorporated the concerns for fiscal integrity in their operations, and the OIGs were therefore at least redundant, and at worst distorting, in their effects on government. In short, the OIGs might cause the government to produce too much accountability at the price of economy and effectiveness.

These hypotheses are helpful because they keep us aware of the possibilities. This, in turn, helps us weigh the evidence of past performance to form conclusions about the present and to make recommendations about how the benefits of the OIGs can be maximized and their risks minimized.

In terms of current performance, we found evidence that was consistent with each of the hypotheses. The balance of the evidence was more supportive of Hypotheses I and II than Hypothesis III. The fact is that there are administrative weaknesses in the organization of federal programs, and there is much that can be done to strengthen them. It also seems likely that the OIGs' enhanced efforts to detect fraud, waste, and abuse, and their capacity to focus (and sometimes follow) media and congressional attention on administrative problems, have strengthened the programs.

At the same time, we found some clear instances in which OIG interventions had important negative consequences for some performance attributes of programs. Consider the following instances from our cases and discussions with program managers:

- A CETA regional manager commented: "We saw a dramatic shift from a focus on program performance—what was happening to the people the money was being spent on—to almost no focus on that or a substantially diminished focus on that coming from the top, to a focus almost exclusively on the issue of how well the money was being managed. We started hearing words that this system hadn't heard in fifteen years."
- Another CETA manager described the impact of audit resolution and debt collection in the following way: "Questioned costs have impacted negatively on peoples' willingness to take risks in program design—to stretch the law and regulations as far as they could to do what they thought made sense in their community."
- A director of a rehabilitation program in the Department of

Labor pointed out that speed and personalized service in getting a physician and therapist to an injured employee were essential for rehabilitation, but that the IG had insisted on using standard federal procurement standards for procuring physician and rehabilitative services. The director's evaluation: "We do not feel it is appropriate to go for the lowest bidder. We need to give personalized service."
- A director of the FmHA Emergency Loan Program, evaluating revised procedures for checking on eligibility proposed by the IG and adopted by management, said: "You know, the word 'emergency' has some significance. . . . Every time you get in an emergency, people want the money out."

These instances are hardly sufficient to declare the OIGs a menace to efficiency in government. But these instances, along with the analytical framework used throughout this investigation, do suggest that an overzealous or narrowminded OIG movement could enhance government accountability at the expense of efficiency.

Recommendations for the Future Development of the Offices of Inspectors-General

It is the crucial importance of making sure that the OIGs contribute to efficiency and performance as well as accountability and program integrity that guides our two principal recommendations for the future development of the OIGs. The first concerns the way that the OIGs should relate to the program managers and the overseers of the government programs. The second concerns methods for making the measurement of efficiency and effectiveness somewhat more objective, or at least more useful so that they can stand against anecdotal evidence of scandal.

RELATIONSHIPS WITH CONGRESS AND PROGRAM MANAGERS

As we have seen, the OIGs are to some degree caught between overseers of government programs, on the one hand, and the program managers, on the other. They are sometimes also caught among competing political overseers with Congress wanting more or less "integrity" than political executives, or with one element of Congress disagreeing with another as to the proper balance to be struck between accountability, administrative costs, and service to clients of programs. The temptation in this situation is for the OIGs to make an alliance with the groups that support their values and their unique contributions most strongly: that is, the groups that emphasize accountability, fiscal integrity, and minimization of fraud, waste, and abuse over all other values. The alternative is for the OIGs to stand with the program managers in their pursuit of economy and efficiency, and a proper balance among the values of accountability, the control of fraud, waste, and abuse, and the delivery of services. In choosing how to position themselves in this complicated set of relationships, we would recommend that the OIGs be guided by the following three principles.

First, the OIGs should understand an important paradox: namely, that their independence and objectivity depend on conflict in these political relationships rather than on their own expertise and knowledge. As noted above, the OIGs must yield to the judgment of political overseers in Congress and political appointees in the executive branch in striking the right balance between the values of accountability, administrative costs, and service to clients. They must also yield to the substantive knowledge of the program managers in making judgments about how measures taken to prevent fraud, waste, and abuse will affect the costs, quantity, and quality of government programs. Consequently, if these groups agree about the administrative character of a program, there is little for the OIGs to do. It is only when they disagree, or when the OIGs can make a plausible argument that they have come up with a proposal which offers a superior balancing of competing values, that the OIGs can make a useful, "independent" contribution. Furthermore, in making their proposals, it is probably wise and useful for the OIGs to include the competing values that are of interest to their partners. That is a potentially useful source of creativity.

Second, the OIGs should make a commitment to the goal of promoting economy and efficiency as the predominant value to be served. Even though they have special responsibilities to serve the goals of accountability, fiscal integrity, and the reduction of fraud, waste, and abuse, as a logical and political matter these goals should yield to the broader goal of promoting economy and efficiency. *This means that some proposals which could enhance accountability and reduce corruption should nonetheless be re-*

jected as inconsistent with overall efficiency. The OIGs should make themselves champions of long-run efficiency above all.

This commitment inevitably draws OIGs into a close working relationship with the program managers who share that goal, which leads to the last and most important principle. The OIGs and program managers should work to develop a relationship in which their shared commitment is to both short-run accountability and long-run performance of public sector programs. This means that the program managers must develop a "tolerance" for the traditional OIG functions of investigation and audit, and for their desire to contribute to the prevention of fraud and abuse and to the promotion of efficiency. Moreover, this tolerance must survive even when the OIG makes technical errors, and political escalations occur. Such things are an inevitable part of managerial life in the public sector. Perhaps more important, however, it means that the OIGs must recognize that the values and methods they represent cannot dominate in the relationship with managers. The OIGs need the managers not only because they must implement the programs, but also because the managers are the only ones in a position to balance interests in minimizing fraud, waste, and abuse; providing a quality service to clients; keeping total administrative costs low; and reporting accurately and reliably to their principals in terms their principals can understand. Since the managers bear the ultimate responsibility for striking the balance among these competing values, their judgment must be dominant in deciding whether to accept OIG proposals unless ordered to do so by political principals. This implies that the OIG may sometimes have to stand between his own staff and political oversight apparatus to give the manager the room necessary to make the proper decision. The relationship will require enormous tact, self-discipline, and technical capacity on both sides to be successful.

TERMS OF ACCOUNTABILITY AND THE MEASUREMENT OF PERFORMANCE

Ultimately, what will make the set of relationships among political overseers, OIGs, and program managers work on behalf of efficiency in public sector programs is for them to reach more or less durable agreements about the terms in which a given program's performance will be measured.[190] In effect, they must decide how to measure the quantity and quality of government services—including measurements of financial integrity and levels of fraud, waste, and abuse. This is essential for determining whether program managers are increasing or decreasing the efficiency of government programs and for evaluating proposed methods to control fraud, waste, and abuse. Obviously, developing a bottom line for government programs has proved elusive. But we think renewed efforts must be made. We recommend that these efforts incorporate the following principles.

First, we think it is important to recognize that government programs have at least two different consumers: those who are the clients of the organization and receive benefits and services (or have obligations imposed) and the general public in whose name the program is launched, whose tax contributions support the program, who might themselves someday become clients of the program, and who want the program to express certain values by having specific operating characteristics. These different groups will respond to different features of the same program. Even when they consider the same features, they won't necessarily value them to the same degree. But the point is that any feature of the program that is important to any of these groups is a candidate for becoming a dimension of performance in which the program should be evaluated. If the clients of the FmHA emergency loan program value the speed of processing, and the political overseers worry about the total costs and geographic distribution of the program, the OIGs and program managers should be prepared to discuss the program in these terms. In effect, the concerns of those interested in a given program should become evaluative dimensions of a program.

Second, *many* measures are probably a better way to evaluate a program's efficacy than any single measure. In the past, we have expended enormous effort to develop a single measure of program effectiveness (for example, the benefit-cost ratio). We have tried to shrink the multidimensionality (and multiclient) character of government programs into a single metric which successfully compares apples to oranges. In doing so, we have paid an enormous price, because we have separated the terms in which government programs are evaluated from the intended goals and purposes of those who authorized the program. The alternative approach would be to relax the requirement for a single measure and rely on multiple measures. This approach is used routinely in the private sector. McDonald's evaluates its franchises not in terms of profits, but in terms of twelve different physical measures of the store's performance (for example, the cleanliness of the restrooms, the time waited in line, and whether the service person smiled).[191] Texas Instruments evaluates its managers not only in terms of short-run operating performance with respect to profits, but also in terms of their success in innovating projects and developing the talents of subordinate personnel.[192] No single metric sums these things: each is measured and discussed.

Third, it may not be necessary to arrive at measures of ultimate value in order for the measures to be valuable in both stimulating and evaluating improvements in efficiency. Again, in the past we have worked hard to develop measures of "outcomes" rather than "outputs." This required analysts to evaluate the effects of government programs on the basis of the ultimate purposes of a program. These ultimate effects generally occurred only far down a causal chain, remote from the boundaries of the government agency. Such program evaluations have been enormously valuable. But we have learned that these measurements are very expensive and cannot be taken often enough or comprehensively enough for them to have managerial value. For a measure to have such value, it must be related to a specific manager, it must be taken at intervals that are short enough to have value as feedback to the manager, it must have some variability, and it must be possible to compare it with benchmarks such as past performance or the performance of other similarly situated programs.[193] Measurements of outcomes fail on all of these criteria: they are difficult to relate to a specific manager; they are rare and intermittent rather than frequent and regular; and they have little variability and few benchmarks. Consequently, to stimulate efficiency and even effectiveness, it may be better to measure valued attributes of outputs rather than outcomes.

In sum, the ultimate challenge for those who run government programs is what it has always been: to establish the terms in which those who manage the program will be accountable to their principals, and to do so in a way that honors the legitimate values and interests of the principals who authorized the program and the clients who are exposed to it. If managers are successful in establishing the appropriate terms of their accountability, there will be no tension between accountability and performance. If, on the other hand, either the principals or the managers are careless in this enterprise, the terms of accountability might distort the government's performance with a loss of some public value that could have been created. Avoiding *that* loss should be the goal of the OIGs, the program managers, and their principals. They should not be diverted by the smaller losses associated with the badly defined but politically powerful concepts of fraud, waste, and abuse.

Notes

[1] The famous quotation from *Federalist 51* sets the tone: "If men were angels, no government would be necessary. If angels were to govern men, neither external nor internal controls on government would be necessary. In framing a government which is to be administered by men over men, the great difficulty lies in this: you must first enable the government to control the governed; and in the next place oblige it to control itself. A dependence on the people is, no doubt, the primary control on the government; but experience has taught mankind the necessity of auxiliary precautions." *The Federalist: Papers by Alexander Hamilton, James Madison, John Jay* (New York: Heritage Press, 1945), p. 348. For a more recent expression of the same sentiments and a link to the General Accounting Office, see Frederick C. Mosher, *The GAO: The Quest for Accountability in American Government* (Boulder, CO: Westover Press, 1979), p. 1.

[2] William Niskanen has developed a theory of bureaucracy whose central premise is a drive for expansion. See "Non-Market Decision-making: The Peculiar Economics of Bureaucracy," *American Economics Review: Papers and Proceedings*, 58 (May 1968): 293–305.

[3] J. Peter Grace has emerged as the most visible spokesman for this position. See *President's Private Sector on Cost Control* (Washington, DC: U.S. Government Printing Office 1983).

[4] Roland McKean, *Efficiency in Government Through Systems Analysis* (New York: Wiley, 1958), chap. 1.

[5] For evidence on the growth in the size and complexity of the government, see Frederick C. Mosher, "The Changing Responsibilities and Tactics of the Federal Government," *Public Administration Review* 40 (November-December 1980):

541–48. For evidence that the President's Council on Integrity and Efficiency (PCIE) shares this diagnosis, see President's Council on Integrity and Efficiency, *Eliminating Fraud, Waste, and Abuse in the Federal Government: A Progress Report to the President, Fiscal Year 1983, Second Six Months* (Washington, DC: PCIE, 1983), pp. 27–28.

[6] See, for example, Anthony Marro, "Fraud in Federal Aid May Exceed $12 Billion Annually, Experts Say," *New York Times*, April 16, 1978, pp. 1 and 26; David Burnham, "U.S. Agencies Starting to Bolster Meager Defenses against Fraud," *New York Times*, April 17, 1978, pp. 1 and 18; and J. Thomas, "Detroit Computer School Is Focus of Case Alleging Cheating in Federal Aid Programs," *New York Times*, April 17, 1978, p. 20.

[7] In the "Fraud, Waste, and Abuse in HEW," David Whitman said that "by the 1980 election, Gallup polls indicated that a majority of Americans believed that government wasted 52 cents out of every dollar it spent." Harvard University, Kennedy School of Government, Case #C14-80-337, 1980, p. 30.

[8] The Inspector-General Act of 1978, Public Law 95-452, 92 Stat. 1101.

[9] "Statement of Edwin L. Harper, Deputy Director, Office of Management and Budget, Before the Intergovernmental Relations and Human Resources Subcommittee of the House of Representatives; On the Inspector-General Program," April 1, 1981, mimeographed.

[10] Mosher, *The GAO*, pp. 43–61.

[11] For a description of the rise of systems analysis and program evaluation in the Department of Defense, see William W. Kaufman, *The McNamara Strategy* (New York: Harper & Row, 1964).

[12] For a discussion of how different aspects of government administrative procedures affect the "quality" of service to clients, see Jeffrey L. Prottas, *People Processing* (Lexington, MA: Heath, 1979).

[13] For a discussion of the legislative history of this Act, see Margaret J. Gates and Marjorie Fine Knowles, "The Inspector General in the Federal Government: A New Approach to Accountability," *Alabama Law Review* 36 (Winter 1985): 473–513.

[14] *United States Code, 1982 Edition* (Washington, DC: U.S. Government Printing Office 1983), p. 987.

[15] The OIG in HEW was created by PL 94-905 and the one in Energy by PL 95-91, section 208. See *Congressional Quarterly Almanac*, vol. 34 (Washington, DC: Congressional Quarterly, 1979), pp. 798–99.

[16] *United States Code: 1982 Edition* (Washington, DC: U.S. Government Printing Office, 1983), p. 987.

[17] The OIG in the Department of State was established by PL 96-465. See *Congressional Quarterly Almanac*, vol. 36 (Washington, DC: Congressional Quarterly, 1981), p. 538.

[18] *Congressional Quarterly Almanac*, vol. 36 (1981), p. 538.

[19] The analysis of the legislative mandate is abstracted from Gates and Knowles, "The Inspector General in the Federal Government." That article was researched as part of this broader project on OIGs.

[20] "Establishment of Offices of Inspector General: Hearings Before a Subcommittee on Governmental Operations," 95th Cong. 1st sess. 1977, 463. [Hereinafter cited as Hearings on H.R. 2819.]

[21] "Memorandum for the President from Griffin Bell regarding H.R. 2819,"

dated February 24, 1977, covering a memorandum for the Attorney General on the same subject from John Harrison dated February 21, 1977.

[22] U.S. Department of Agriculture, "Secretary's Memorandum No. 1503" (June 25, 1962).

[23] Comptroller General of the United States, *Report to the Congress: Review of Activities of the Inspector General, Department of Agriculture*, 95th Cong., 2d sess., May 8, 1968.

[24] Ibid., p. 6.

[25] Ralph M. Huppert, "The Inspector General Concept in Federal Law Enforcement" (unpublished seminar paper by an employee of the OIG at Department of Agriculture).

[26] "Establishment of an Office of Inspector General in the Department of Health, Education and Welfare: Hearings on H.R. 5302 Before a Sub-Committee of the House Committee on Governmental Operations," 94th Cong., 2d sess., 1976, 2. [Hereinafter cited as Hearings on H.R. 5302.]

[27] Ibid.

[28] Senate Special Committee on Aging, "Background Materials Relating to the Office of Inspector General, Department of Health and Human Services," 97th Cong., 1st sess., 1981, 6–7. [Hereinafter cited as Background Materials.]

[29] Ibid.

[30] Gates and Knowles, "The Inspector General in the Federal Government" pp. 488–89.

[31] Ibid., fn. 21.

[32] United States Code, Title 5: Appendix, Inspector-General Act of 1978, sections 5(a), 5(b), and 5(d).

[33] See, for example, the *New York Times*, September 19, 1978, concerning fraud at the General Services Administration, and hearings held by Senator Lawton Chiles, Chair of the Senate Subcommittee on Federal Spending Practices. See also, *Associated Press Supplementary Material* (September 19, 1978), p. 78.

[34] *Congressional Quarterly Almanac*, vol. 34 (1978), pp. 798–99.

[35] The growth in resources has not yet occurred, but the IGs have been effective in avoiding budget cuts. House of Representatives, "Oversight of Offices of Inspector General: Hearings Before a Sub-Committee of the Committee of Government Operations," 97th Cong., 1st sess., April 1 and June 10, 1981 (Washington, DC: U.S. Government Printing Office, 1981), pp. 27–28.

[36] United States Code, Title 5: Appendix, Inspector-General Act of 1978, sections 3(d)(1) and 3(d)(2).

[37] Ibid., section 3(a).

[38] Ibid., section 3(a).

[39] Ibid., section 3(a).

[40] Ibid., section 4(a)(5).

[41] Ibid., section 5(d); sections 5(a) and 5(b).

[42] Ibid., section 5(d)(2).

[43] Hearings on H.R. 2819.

[44] Inspector-General Act of 1978.

[45] Esther Scott, "The Inspector General and the Farmer's Home Administration," Harvard University, Kennedy School of Government, Case #C15-82-486, 1982, pp. 4–12.

[46] Whitman, "Fraud, Waste, and Abuse in HEW," p. 10.

[47] Scott, "The IG and the FmHA," p. 9.

[48] Robert Leavitt, "The Inspector General at the Department of Labor," Harvard University, Kennedy School of Government, Case #C15-82-487, 1982, pp. 27–28.

[49] Scott, "The IG and the FmHA," pp. 18–26.

[50] Ibid., p. 28.

[51] For an extended discussion of these difficulties, see Herbert Kaufman, *Red Tape: Its Origins, Uses and Abuses* (Washington, DC: Brookings Institution, 1977), pp. 5–22.

[52] In the Department of Labor, typically only about one third of the questioned costs were ultimately identified as wasteful expenditures. Leavitt, "The IG at the DOL," p. 14.

[53] William J. Lanouette, "IGs Say an Ounce of Prevention May Save Billions for Their Agencies," *National Journal* (June 19, 1982), pp. 1094–97.

[54] For a discussion of administrative controls, see Office of Management and Budget, "Guidelines for the Evaluation and Improvement of Internal Control Systems in the Federal Government," February 24, 1982, mimeographed.

[55] Ibid.

[56] Scott, "The IG and the FmHA."

[57] It is interesting that FmHA stopped making certain kinds of loans in its Emergency Loan Program following IG investigations: that is, those for "major adjustments" or "annual production" rather than "actual losses" due to national disasters. See Scott, "The IG and the FmHA," pp. 4–12. It is also interesting that CETA cut back its Public Sector Employment Program radically. See Leavitt, "The IG at the DOL," p. 17.

[58] Scott, "The IG and the FmHA," p. 7.

[59] This was proposed as a way of lowering "error rates" in the welfare program. See David Jernigan, "Controlling AFDC Error Rates," Harvard University, Kennedy School of Government, Case #C14-80-302, 1980.

[60] This was proposed. See Robert Leavitt, "The Inspector General and the Food Stamp Program—Summary," Harvard University, Kennedy School of Government, 1981, pp. 8–9.

[61] Ibid., fn. 57.

[62] Our cases provided numerous instances of press leaks of IG reports. In particular, see Scott, "The IG and the FmHA," p. 22, which describes a press leak of an IG audit report on the "gasohol" loans.

[63] "Statement of John P. White, Deputy Director of OMB Before the Legislation and National Security Subcommittee of the Committee on Government Operation of the House of Representatives on H.R. 7893, a Bill to Amend the Inspector General Act of 1978," in "Inspector General Act Amendments of 1980: Hearings Before a Subcommittee of the Committee of Government Operations, House of Representatives," 96th Cong., August 27–28, 1980. [Hereinafter cited as Hearings on H.R. 7893.]

[64] Ibid., pp. 46–47.

[65] This was a consequence of having it chaired by the Deputy AG and having relatively little White House attention given to it.

[66] Hearings on H.R. 7893, p. 49.

[67] Ibid., p. 48.

[68] Report of the Attorney General, *National Priorities for the Investigation and Prosecution of White Collar Crime* (Washington, DC: Department of Justice, 1980).

[69] Diane Curtis, "Wasting No Time in Clearing His Administration of Democratic Appointees, President Reagan, Wednesday, Fired Most of the Nation's Inspectors General," UPI, *Washington News,* January 21, 1981.

[70] "Statement of Edwin L. Harper before the Intergovernmental Relations and Human Resources Community," April 1, 1981, p. 4.

[71] Ibid.

[72] See note 69. " 'We want people who are meaner than a junkyard dog at ferreting out fraud, waste and mismanagement,' said press secretary James Brady."

[73] Ronald Reagan, "Executive Order: Integrity and Efficiency in Federal Programs," March 26, 1981.

[74] Ibid.

[75] White House, "Reform 88 Press Release," September 22, 1982.

[76] Interview with Charles Dempsey, September 10, 1982. [Hereinafter cited as Dempsey interview.]

[77] PCIE, *Eliminating Fraud, Waste and Abuse,* p. 1.

[78] Ibid., p. 3.

[79] Ibid., pp. 14–19.

[80] Ibid. fn. 38.

[81] Interview with Thomas Morris, September 13, 1982. [Hereinafter cited as Morris interview.] Interview with Kurt Muellenberg, July 13, 1982. [Hereinafter cited as Muellenberg interview.]

[82] Morris interview.

[83] Muellenberg interview.

[84] Interview with Marjorie Knowles, October 12, 1982. [Hereinafter cited as Knowles interview.]

[85] Interview with Ronald Goldstock, December 1982. [Hereinafter cited as Goldstock interview.]

[86] Interview with Thomas McBride, August 15, 1982. [Hereinafter cited as McBride interview.]

[87] Interview with John Graziano, August 31, 1982. [Hereinafter cited as Graziano interview.]

[88] McBride interview.

[89] Ibid.

[90] Leavitt, "The IG at the DOL," pp. 4–5.

[91] Ibid., p. 5.

[92] Interviews with Goldstock, Morris, McBride, and Graziano. See also Whitman, "Fraud, Waste, and Abuse in HEW."

[93] Goldstock interview.

[94] "Internal Control Systems," OMB Circular no. A-123 (Washington, DC: OMB, 1981).

[95] PCIE, *Eliminating Fraud, Waste, and Abuse,* pp. 21–22.

[96] Interviews with Muellenberg, Knowles, McBride, and Morris.

[97] McBride interview. Also interview with Joseph Sikon, September 9, 1982. [Hereinafter cited as Sikon interview.]

[98] Graziano interview. Also interview with Richard Kusserow, September 1, 1982. [Hereinafter cited as Kusserow interview.]

[99] PCIE, "Inspection Activities of the Inspectors General: Draft Report," August 1984, mimeographed.

[100] Ibid., p. 1.

[101] Ibid.

[102] Ibid.

[103] See, in particular, interviews with Kusserow and Dempsey.

[104] Dempsey interview.

[105] Interview with Bryan Mitchell, September 1, 1982. [Hereinafter cited as Mitchell interview.]

[106] Frank Sato, remark at a conference of IGs and Program Managers, January 21, 1983.

[107] Muellenberg interview.

[108] McBride interview.

[109] Muellenberg interview.

[110] McBride interview.

[111] Dempsey interview.

[112] McBride interview.

[113] Muellenberg interview.

[114] Goldstock interview.

[115] Kusserow interview.

[116] Dempsey interview.

[117] Graziano interview.

[118] McBride interview.

[119] Morris interview.

[120] McBride interview.

[121] Dempsey interview.

[122] Ibid.

[123] Muellenberg interview; Sikon interview.

[124] Sikon interview.

[125] Goldstock interview.

[126] McBride interview.

[127] Goldstock interview.

[128] Dempsey interview.

[129] Goldstock interview.

[130] Ibid.

[131] Sikon interview.

[132] Ibid.

[133] Dempsey interview.

[134] Ibid.

[135] McBride interview.

[136] Ibid.

[137] Ibid.

[138] Dempsey interview.
[139] Ibid.
[140] Morris Interview.
[141] Goldstock interview.
[142] For an extended discussion of the concept of "accountability," see Appendix A: The Concept of Accountability.
[143] The crucial cases on which we relied were Whitman, "Fraud, Waste, and Abuse in HEW"; Scott, "The IG and the FmHA"; Leavitt, "The IG at the DOL"; Jernigan, "Controlling AFDC Error Rates"; Leavitt, "The IG and the Food Stamp Program—Summary."
[144] Two meetings were held in Washington, DC on January 21, 1983. The attendees were the following: Joan Claybrook, for the Administration of the National Highway Traffic Safety Administration; Charles A. Dempsey, Inspector-General at the Department of Housing and Urban Development; Edward Elmendorf, Acting Assistant Secretary for Student Financial Assistance, Department of Education; Robert Greenstein, Director of the Center on Budget and Policy Priorities and former official in the Department of Agriculture; David Russ, Assistant to the Assistant Secretary for Human Development Services, Department of Health and Human Services; Steve Hitchner, Vice President, Common Cause; Jim Moriarity, Assistant to the Administrator of Financial Control and Management Systems, Department of Labor; John McClellan, Associate Director of the Federal Employees Compensation, Department of Labor; Thomas Morris, Consultant to the National Institute of Public Affairs, formerly Inspector-General of the Department of Health, Education, and Welfare; Frank Sato, Inspector-General of the Veterans Administration; James Schoenberger, Associate Deputy Assistant Secretary, Multi-Family Housing Programs, Department of Housing and Urban Development; James B. Thomas, Jr., Inspector General, Department of Education; James B. Thornton, President of JAC Corporation, formerly with the Farmer's Home Administration; Joseph P. Welsh, Inspector-General with the Department of Transportation; Jack Corrigan, Assistant to the Deputy Assistant Secretary for Economic Development, Department of Commerce.
[145] PCIE, *Eliminating Fraud, Waste, and Abuse*, p. 11.
[146] McBride interview.
[147] Kusserow interview.
[148] Leavitt, "The IG at the DOL," pp. 15–16.
[149] Ibid., p. 5.
[150] Ibid., pp. 22–24.
[151] Scott, "The IG and the FmHA," p. 16.
[152] PCIE, "Inspection Activities."
[153] PCIE, *Eliminating Fraud, Waste, and Abuse*, p. 8.
[154] PCIE, "Inspection Activities," pp. 5–7.
[155] PCIE, *Eliminating Fraud, Waste, and Abuse*, p. 11.
[156] Ibid., p. 9.
[157] Ibid., p. 10.
[158] See, generally, Leavitt, "The IG at the DOL," pp. 2–18.
[159] Ibid., p. 2.

[160] Ibid., p. 6.
[161] Ibid., p. 7.
[162] Ibid., p. 7.
[163] Ibid., p. 7.
[164] Ibid., p. 9.
[165] Ibid., p. 9.
[166] Ibid., p. 10.
[167] Ibid., p. 9.
[168] Ibid., pp. 12–13.
[169] Ibid., p. 13.
[170] Ibid., p. 13.
[171] Ibid., p. 13. For a similar story in a different program, see Whitman, "Fraud, Waste, and Abuse in HEW."
[172] Whitman, p. 14.
[173] PCIE, Addressing Fraud, Waste, and Abuse: A Summary Report of Inspector General Activities (Washington, DC: PCIE, 1981).
[174] PCIE, Eliminating Fraud, Waste, and Abuse, p. 7.
[175] Leavitt, "The IG and the Food Stamp Program," pp. 5–6.
[176] Ibid., p. 7.
[177] Leavitt, "The IG at the DOL," pp. 27–28.
[178] Scott, "The IG and the FmHA," pp. 7–12.
[179] Leavitt, "The IG and the Food Stamp Program," p. 5.
[180] Leavitt, "The IG at the DOL," pp. 25–27.
[181] See, in particular, the long-run evolution of the CETA Program, the Food Stamp Program, and the FmHA Business and Industrial Loan Program—all of which have improved as a result of combined IG, program manager, congressional, and local agency collaboration.
[182] Leavitt, "The IG at the DOL," pp. 22–24.
[183] Scott, "The IG and the FmHA," pp. 14–29.
[184] Leavitt, "The IG at the DOL," pp. 25–27.
[185] Ibid., pp. 22–23.
[186] Whitman, "Fraud, Waste, and Abuse at HEW," pp. 22–30.
[187] Leavitt, "The IG at the DOL," p. 30.
[188] Ibid.
[189] For an extended discussion, see Appendix A: The Concept of Accountability.
[190] This is consistent with recommendations made by Peat, Marwick, and Mitchell. See Paul K. Brace, Robert Elkin, Daniel D. Robinson, and Harold I. Steinberg, Reporting on Service Efforts and Accomplishments (Stanford, CT: Finanacial Accounting Standards Board, 1980).
[191] "The McDonald Corporation," Harvard University, Harvard Business School, Case #9-681-044.
[192] "Texas Instruments: Management Systems," Harvard University, Harvard Business School, Case #172-054.
[193] Robert N. Anthony and Regina Herzlinger, Management Control in Nonprofit Organizations (Homewood, IL: Irwin, 1975), chap. 2, pp. 16–34.

Appendix A   The Concept of Accountability

The issue of accountability arises in situations in which a "principal" exists who has resources and purposes, but entrusts the resources to an agent to carry out his purposes.[1] The principal may choose to rely on the agent because the agent has a specialized competence, some particular knowledge, or simply more time to spend on the project. Whatever the reasons, the principal quite naturally wants to be sure that the agent will carry out these purposes reliably. Consequently, he selects an agent whose reputation is consistent with good performance and honest reporting of accomplishments and whose promises with respect to the principal's current purposes suggest a high degree of competence.

Mere protestations of good will, competence, and integrity, however, will not ordinarily satisfy the principal. He wants more assurances that the agent is advancing the principal's purposes rather than his own. To satisfy himself that this is the case, the principal will impose terms on the agent's performance. The agent will be required to achieve some ultimate grand purpose, to achieve specific objectives, to engage in certain activities, or to use resources in a particular way. In addition, the agent will be required to file regular reports on his activities and to accept the scrutiny and inspection of the principal. Moreover, the principal may establish the opportunity to renegotiate or even terminate the contract if the agent's reports (or the principal's inspections) reveal difficulties. In general, the more suspicious the principal is of the agent, the more exacting the terms of the contract will be.

However, there must be limits to the principal's interests in instructing, monitoring, and renegotiating with the agent. If the principal spends so much time thinking about how to do a job, checking to see that it is done well, and worrying about whether things are going as planned, he might as well leave the agent out altogether. This is true even if the constant "micro-management" has no impact on the motivations and capacities of the agent. If the persistent reviews waste the agent's time and sap his motivation and creativity as well, then the point at which suspicion becomes counterproductive comes even sooner in terms of the amount of reassurance the principal requires.[2]

From the perspective of the principal, then, establishing terms of accountability with respect to the agent serves several important functions. It allows him to give the agent more or less particular and more or less permanent instructions about what he wants the agent to do and how he wants him to do it. It allows him to ascertain (and investigate at his initiative) if the agent is serving his interests. And it gives him a device for motivating— even requiring—the agent to perform his duties. Taken together, these features give the principal an exceedingly valuable opportunity—*the opportunity to give attention to something other than the details of the agent's performance*. In effect, the terms of accountability provide the principal with enough assurances that the agent is doing his job well to be able to avoid doing the job himself, and, instead, to concentrate on other things.

From the point of view of the agent, accountability means staying within the terms of the contract established by the principal. To a degree, his responsibilities are fully defined by the literal terms of the contract. If he stays within the substantive and reporting terms, we may say he is fully accountable. But often the literal terms are more properly understood as indicative of broad responsibilities than narrowly limited and exacting duties. Sometimes this is true because the terms of the contract are themselves quite general. This need not be the result of sloppiness, but instead to leave room for the agent to use his special expertise. After all, if the principal knew exactly what to do to achieve his purposes, he probably wouldn't need the agent. But even if the terms are quite narrow, the principal may prefer that the agent ignore the literal terms if he can imagine a better way of accomplishing a particular goal. Or the agent may spot an opportunity for long-term improvements by violating some short-term conditions of his accountability. In short, both the principal and the agent may assume that the agent has a *general* duty to advance the interests of the principal beyond the narrow terms of their explicit contract.[3] Indeed, they may even agree that violations of the literal terms would be not only justifiable, but obligatory if such violations were in the short- or long-run interest of the principal.

Different Dimensions of the Accountability Relationship

The contract established between principal and agent has many different characteristics relevant to describing the nature of the accountability that is established.

THE SPECIFICITY OF THE CONTRACT

One characteristic already mentioned is the specificity of the "contract." In general, the more detailed the contract in terms of aims, methods, and uses of resources, the less discretion the agent has. This is obviously desirable if the principal knows exactly what he wants and distrusts the agent. It is less desirable if the principal is more dependent on the agent for his ability to give broad aims concrete existence or if the principal trusts the agent. And it is almost certainly true that no matter how narrowly the contract is written, the agent will have some degree of irreducible discretion, if for no other reason than that his conduct is hard to monitor and observe.[4]

ACCOUNTABILITY FOR OUTCOMES, OUTPUTS, PROCESSES, OR RESOURCES

A second important feature of the contract establishing the terms of accountability between principal and agent is the focus of the contract in terms of *stages of production,* from the granting of fungible resources to the production of final value. Table

A.1 offers some examples of these different stages of production for government programs dealing with crime, poverty, and environmental protection. Contracts can be established to hold agents accountable at any of these stages. Some will be established primarily in terms of *outcomes:* that is, the agent is held accountable for achieving a purpose without much specification as to means. An example would be to hold a police commissioner responsible for reducing violent crime. Other contracts are established primarily in terms of *outputs:* the agent is responsible for producing a tangible product, an activity, or result which is intermediate to the production of the ultimate values. An example might be holding a police commissioner responsible for increasing the number of arrests or responding to calls for service within a certain amount of time. Still others can be drawn in terms of the required use of technologies or operating procedures: the agent is responsible for using resources according to rules that define the best professional practices, not necessarily for achieving a particular goal whether intermediate or final. For example, a police commissioner might be responsible for committing a certain portion of his resources to random patrol and for having a modern communication system as specified by a professional association such as the International Association of Chiefs of Police. In still other contracts, the agent is responsible for nothing more than being able to either apply the resources in appropriate ways or account for their location. Indeed, since virtually all principal-agent relations require some accounting for the receipt and use of resources, the principal difference among accounting schemes is whether they also measure specific procedures through which the resources are combined and the quantity and quality of outputs produced or the achievement of ultimate goals.

Often the generality of the terms in which agents are held accountable is confused with the stage of production for which they are accountable. Narrow specificity is often associated with measurement of procedures and outputs, while broad generalities are linked to measurement of outcomes. Logically, this need not be the case. One could use quite vague language to describe technologies (for example, "best available methods") and quite detailed language to describe outcomes (for example, reduce the parts per million of particulate matter in the air from 0.00100 to 0.00025 for 360 days in the year). As a practical matter, however,

Table A.1 Different Points of Control Within Government Programs

Functional Areas	Available Resources	Stages of Production		
		Existing Technologies/ Operating Procedures	Outputs	Outcomes
Police/Crime	Policemen	Geographical definition of patrol sectors	Response time to calls for service	Reduced crime Arrests
	Police cars	Priorities for dispatching patrol cars		Increased security Reduced economic cost
Welfare/Poverty	Caseworkers Welfare offices	Procedures for eligibility determination and benefit calculation	Case decisions: speed, accuracy, fairness	Reduced poverty Increased confidence in administrative integrity Reduced economic cost
Environmental Protection	Inspectors	Installation of Anti-pollution technologies	Reduced effluents	Clean air & water
	Research on health effects	Compliance actions by government		Net effects on economic development

these two features of accountability are often closely linked. The reason is that resources, activities, and outputs all exist within (or at) the boundaries of an organizational unit. Consequently, they can all be observed and accounted for more readily than *outcomes*, which are likely to occur in a place beyond the boundaries of the organization and at a time in the future rather than now. It is also true that activities and outputs happen before outcomes and that managers often have greater control over the conditions that lead to them than they do over outcomes. In effect, the causal route to outcomes includes a great many interacting variables that take time to operate, and only some of them are under the manager's control. To the extent that the goal of a system of accountability is to hold agents accountable only for what they control and provide prompt information about their performance, then that system should monitor procedures, activities, and outputs rather than outcomes.[5]

Table A.2 gives examples of more or less specific terms of accountability established at different stages of production. In general, the narrowest terms of accountability—the ones that give the agents the least scope for their own initiative—are in the top left corner of the figure. The broadest forms of accountability— the ones that give the agents the greatest scope by virtue of the principal's confidence or need—are those at the lower right. For the most part, government tends to establish accountability in terms of specific activity rather than general outcome which requires greater trust. The private sector seems to operate with specific outcome responsibilities, which leave agents with broad discretion as to means but quite narrow obligations as to accomplishments.

MONITORING PERFORMANCE

A third important characteristic of an accountability relationship is the way in which performance will be monitored. One dimension is how often performance is monitored. It could be annually or weekly, on a fixed schedule, or at the whim of the principal. A second important dimension is who will monitor. Ordinarily, the agent is responsible for keeping records and compiling reports that characterize his performance in terms set out in the contract. The principal often hires someone to verify the reports. Sometimes the verification is done only on the basis of ex-

Table A.2 Terms of Accountability by Stage of Production

Level of Generality	Stage of Production		
	Process	Output	Outcome
Specific			
Policing	Deploy two-man patrol cars to each sector	Respond to all calls for service in less than five minutes	Surveys of citizen satisfaction show increase of 10% in "favorable" ratings
Environmental Protection	Install "scrubbers" in steel industry	Reduce SO_2 emissions by 10%	Meet standards 95% of the time for ambient condition of air for SO_2
General			
Policing	Maintain a mixed force of motorized patrol, foot patrol, and detectives	Meet citizen demands for service in decently responsive way	Enhance citizen security
Environmental Protection	Promote industrial efforts to clean environment	Abate pollution	Produce a safe and clean environment

isting records; at other times the records are checked against some external reality. The verification can also be more or less comprehensive. Sometimes only a sample of records is examined; at other times the review is more complete. A third important feature of monitoring is whether it will be conducted before or after operational decisions are made, and if after, how long after. Some systems require activities by the agent to be authorized in advance by the principal. Other systems look at the agent's performance only in retrospect—sometimes long after the events occurred. Obviously, the more frequently performance is examined, the more thoroughly records are checked, and the quicker the appraisal of actions, the more exacting is the structure of accountability.

THE LIABILITY OF THE AGENT

A final important feature of accountability is the personal liability of the agent—that is, the character and magnitude of the penalties associated with failures to live up to the rules of the contract and the rules that govern when and how they are applied. To a degree, a formal structure of accountability could, by itself, influence the behavior of agents. If the agents were well motivated, or if they were mindful of their future reputation, then the principal's guidance alone might motivate compliance. Ordinarily, however, we assume that structures of accountability need personal liability, punishments, and rewards in order to be effective.[6] Thus, fixing accountability on individuals, and rewarding them for successful performance, is an important aspect of accountability. The penalties and rewards can be large or small, more or less frequently applied, and more or less easy for the principal to invoke.

THE SPIRIT OF THE RELATIONSHIP

There are certain inevitable tensions in both the spirit and the details of accountability relationships. Many people are accustomed to thinking of accountability primarily as a question of obligating the agent to do what the principal wants. When we think in these terms, we are apt to think of building tight boxes around the agent: the terms of the contract are narrowly specified; provisions are made for frequent, close, and independent monitoring;

the focus of the contract is on the use of resources and the achievement of proximate objectives in order to keep the agent continually mindful of his responsibilities; and the penalties or rewards are large and swiftly and easily invoked.

Another way of thinking about the structure of accountability is that the principal *needs* the agent's knowledge and efforts to achieve his purposes precisely because he is a bit vague about what he wants and how it might be accomplished. When we think in these terms, we are likely to structure accountability in quite different ways. The contract will be cast in more general or abstract terms to allow for invention and change, its focus might be on ultimate purposes rather than the application of resources through well-known methods, and the character of the reporting and dialogue between the principal and the agent will be quite different. There is still an accountability *relationship*—the agent still owes the principal performance—but the *terms* of the relationship are significantly different. The proper form of accountability between principal and agent will depend crucially on what each knows and can contribute to the other and on the degree of trust that exists between them.

Accountability in the Public Sector

Obviously, this is an abstract characterization of the concept of accountability—one that would be just as appropriate for describing the relationship between stockholders and financiers in private sector firms vis-à-vis their executives as it is for the relationship between the overseers of public sector enterprises and their executives. But using the private sector as a comparison within the same abstract terms allows us to see where and how problems might arise in structuring accountability in the public sector.

AMBIGUITY ABOUT THE PRINCIPAL AND THE PURPOSES

One obvious problem is discerning the principals: who are they and what are their goals? A starting point is to assume that Congress is the principal, and the managers of specific programs authorized by Congress are the agents. The implied contract between them consists, in the first instance, of the statutes under which the agency or program operates. The statutes include both *authorizing legislation* (which typically establishes broad purposes described in high levels of abstraction and survives unchanged for long periods of time) and *appropriations bills* (which emphasize means, are written at much lower levels of abstraction, and change annually). In addition to these statutes, however, understandings may be established in legislative oversight hearings or in special congressional investigations which explicate, perhaps even modify, the existing terms of the contract between Congress and the agency.[7]

In theory, of course, Congress speaks with one voice to executive branch agencies. In practice, however, there is often disagreement within Congress over the goals and methods of various programs. Indeed, the current structure of subcommittees offers many different institutional salients from which dissident representatives can advance their particular views against others.[8] And the strength of different congressional voices waxes and wanes over time. So, at any given moment, the mandate under which public agencies operate may depend on whose voice in Congress is the loudest and most recent.

As if this were not trouble enough, our constitutional system creates a second principal in the form of elected political executives and the people whom they appoint to carry out their policies. These political executives also establish terms of accountability in the form of policy pronouncements, budgets, and new procedures.[9] While these terms of accountability often overlap with those established by Congress, enough discrepancies usually exist to keep the lines of communication among the political executives and interested congressional committees quite active and the lines between public executives and their two principals quite confused.

The courts, too, might be considered principals, but their responsibilities are narrower and their interventions more sporadic than those of Congress and political executives.[10] And in the background of many discussions of agency performance is the conventional wisdom of the experts who have standing in given areas of policy, and the media which mete out praise and blame. These factors, too, may sometimes set some of the terms in which public sector managers feel accountable to the public.[11]

In sum, in the real world of the public sector, there may be no single principal with a well-defined purpose. Instead, there are several institutions that feel entitled to set policy and to have the public sector executives be accountable to them and their purposes. Among these principals, there may be a conflict over both means and ends. There may also be conflict over the very terms of accountability, with some interested in broad, infrequent oversight and others much more interested in the "micro-management" of the agencies. Moreover, the principals may often change their minds about either the substance or form of accountability. Thus, the terms of accountability are always changing—becoming focused more on one goal than another, becoming broader or narrower, and becoming more or less insistent depending on political vagaries and media coverage. Over time, conflict and frequent changes in the terms of accountability threaten the commitment of the executives to their overseers, for it seems that there is nothing they can do to satisfy them and no investment seems worth making. At that stage, both accountability and performance are threatened.

PROBLEMS IN MEASUREMENT

A second major problem for accountability in the public sector is the problem of measuring performance. In the private sector, accountability is established primarily in terms of revenues, costs, and profits. Perhaps too much is made of the private sector's reliance on the bottom line. After all, the bottom line refers only to past performance, and all the important decisions to be made are about the future. Consequently, in the best-managed private firms, bottom line responsibility does not exhaust a manager's responsibilities.[12] In addition to meeting annual profit objectives, managers may be responsible for making investments in future capacities to perform or for developing personnel in their organizations.[13] They might even be responsible for meeting certain activity or output objectives independent of revenues.[14] Measurement of these dimensions of performance is as difficult in the private sector as it is in the public sector because it involves subjective judgments about what in the future might have value rather than an objective measurement of what actually has produced value in the past. In spite of these problems, it is nonetheless clear that earning revenues that are tied to overall levels of output and systematically relating them to the costs of production in standard accounting systems do give the private sector an advantage in measuring performance. Moreover, a long tradition of accounting in the private sector both justifies and equips organizations to measure costs, revenues, and profits easily and accurately and provides them with a rich historical data base against which to measure current performance.

The public sector faces more serious difficulties in measuring its performance in terms that satisfy its principals. The central problem is that there is nothing like a revenue paid by customers that measures the private value of public sector production. There are, of course, the ultimate purposes of government such as the defense of America, the preservation and production of clean air and water, the deterrence and rehabilitation of criminal offenders, and the provision of assistance to those who are victims of natural and social disasters. But exactly how much particular organizations contribute to these broad objectives *and what the achievement of these objectives would be worth to the society* remain obscure despite investments in elaborate techniques to evaluate the outcomes of government programs and to determine their value.[15] As a result, the public sector has been reduced to measuring outputs or activities of its organizations: for example, the combat readiness of military units, the reduction of industrial effluents, or the arrests of offenders. It is as though General Motors had to determine whether it was creating social value (that is, being profitable) by looking at its costs and counting the number of cars it builds rather than by examining the revenues it earns from selling the cars. Indeed, the public sector has often been forced to retreat even further from the practice of holding agents accountable for the production of final outcomes. They have eschewed measurement of output in favor of measuring whether resources are used properly in specific production processes: for example, whether a military unit is staffed and organized in a particular way, whether a certain kind of pollution control technology has been installed, whether patrol cars are assigned according to particular spatial configurations, or whether benefit programs are administered in particular ways. A comparable situation in the private sector would require General Motors to assess its profitability by examining whether the specified amount of labor and materials are applied to the production of the automobiles they manufacture without noticing the characteristics of the cars, let alone the revenues that the cars earn.

Thus, the traditional measure of government performance—the

line-item budget—focuses principally on how resources are being used. There is generally less detail on the quantity or quality of government output, and the measurement of outcomes is rare indeed. Moreover, since the capacity of a measurement system to guide behavior depends a great deal on its historical use (which legitimates the system and establishes benchmarks against which current performance can be measured), the real capacity of the newer measurement systems that focus on outcomes or outputs to guide public sector production is even less than their sporadic use would indicate, for even when used they lack power. As a result, measurement systems in the public sector drive public executives to emphasize the process of production rather than outputs or outcomes.

THIRD PARTY PRODUCTION

A third problem for accountability in the public sector, and particularly for the federal government, is that much of the production for which it is accountable (in either process or output terms) is carried out by relatively independent organizations. Welfare, food stamps, medicaid, and compensatory education are all programs financed by the federal government, but implemented primarily by local government units.[16] Similarly, regulatory programs in the areas of environmental protection, mine safety, occupational safety and health, and even equal opportunity are carried out by organizations that operate independently of the government and have much different objectives. Of course, the local government units and private sector organizations are legally accountable to the federal government through the structure of laws and regulations that impose duties on them and that are monitored by regular systems of reporting and inspection as well as through complaints brought by the general public. In this sense they are not wholly independent: they must meet their legal obligation to the federal government.

The point is, however, that the structural and political independence of the different units blunts the structure of accountability that is created. The independent units do not think of themselves as the agents of the federal government, and they have enough legal and political power to operate with relative independence in deciding what they will do and when and how they will report.[17] Consequently, the literal terms of each unit's accountability tend to establish the *maximum* terms of their accountability rather than the minimum, which might be the case if these units were joined in a single organization. This is particularly true if the local units do not share the objectives of the federal government.[18] Even if the local units do share federal government objectives, they may feel relatively little obligation to fulfill federal regulations and reporting requirements. As a result, any given level of administrative effort exerted by the federal government will probably exact less compliance and produce less accountability among the independent organizations than it would if the organizations were truly subordinate to the federal government. Moreover, since the federal program managers understand that they are vulnerable to being undercut through political back channels if they press too hard, they feel less responsible for achieving their goals than they otherwise would.[19]

One further consequence of this indirect relationship is worth noting. From the point of view of Congress, the federal official who is responsible for the program is a line manager. Congress expects the Administrator of the Elementary and Secondary School Education Program to produce the results it mandated when it passed the law creating the program.[20] Congress may also feel entitled, then, to establish an additional staff organization such as an Inspector-General, a General Accounting Office, or an Office of Planning and Evaluation to review the performance of this federal line manager.

From the point of view of the local school boards, however, the federal program manager hardly seems like a superior line manager. His job is simply to check that the local school board performs a certain number of specific tasks to which it is committed by the terms of its grant. In this, the federal manager resembles an overseeing audit organization rather than a superior line manager. The superior line manager would be someone who could stand for the broadest purposes of the organization and could guarantee the future of those who worked for the organization. They would establish this relationship to local units of government rather than to the federal government. Thus, from the perspective of those actually implementing the programs, the federal line manager and the Inspector-General who oversees the federal line manager appear to be performing the same function: that of checking to make sure that the local units are living up to their minimal responsibilities to the federal government. In short, the indirect relationship produces redundant levels of oversight due to confusion about who is the line manager and who is responsible for checking on the narrower interests of the federal government.

INNOVATIVE PROGRAMS

A fourth feature of the current situation that confounds simple notions of accountability is that many government programs are new. In trying to clean the air and water, promote equality of educational opportunity, or even give out food stamps and welfare benefits to eligible populations decently and accurately, there is much to be learned. While the government is learning to perform these tasks, performance inevitably varies.

In the private sector, variability in methods and performance would be taken as a virtue since it would signal innovation and provide the opportunity to learn about more effective methods of production. Some of the experiments would, of course, be failures, but others would be quite successful, and the failures would be understood as the necessary price of the success. In the public sector, however, variability in performance is generally treated as a problem. Part of the reason is that everyone expects the government to know what it is doing before it goes into a new business. If there is some uncertainty about whether and how the government can be successful in a new enterprise, then it is the opinion of many that the government should stay out of that business: government shouldn't gamble with tax dollars.

Another part of the problem, however, is an interest in uniformity and equity in the imposition of burdens and the granting of benefits.[21] Fairness means that like cases should be treated alike. Diversity and innovation in government operations mean that like cases are treated differently. Thus, expectations that the government can be accountable only by doing exactly what it said it would do in advance, and by treating all cases alike, come into conflict with the fact that many of the government's programs are new and require experimentation and learning.

In this situation, one of two things will happen: the pursuit of narrow accountability will frustrate the potential for learning or accounting systems based on compliance with preannounced procedures will conclude inaccurately that the government programs are failing. The only way to avoid this result is by setting out the terms of accountability in broader language that leaves room for innovation and learning. But the broad policy guidance also leaves a great deal of discretion in the hands of public sector executives.

SANCTIONS FOR PERFORMANCE

A fifth issue of accountability in the public sector concerns the sanctions to be imposed on public officials if they fail to meet their responsibilities. The common view is that public officials are much less "accountable" than private sector managers because civil service rules—originally established to prevent political patronage—now shield public officials from sanctions for poor performance. Since public managers cannot easily be fired, demoted, or have their salaries trimmed (nor for that matter be easily promoted or granted raises), there is insufficient accountability in the public sector.[22]

To a degree, the conventional view is accurate. Almost certainly there is less variability in salaries and rates of promotion in public sector bureaucracies than in private sector companies, and therefore fewer economic incentives to be manipulated. But variability in economic rewards is only one element of a powerful system of accountability. The other elements we have already mentioned: continuity in the substantive purposes of the relationship, accurate (or at least convincing) measurement of performance, and a continuing personal relationship that gives concrete expression to the continuity in the overall goals and objectives. In these dimensions the differences between public and private sector operations may be the greatest.

One of the areas of greatest change in the public sector is in leadership. The average tenure of political appointees is less than two years.[23] This would not be a problem if there were a broad consensus about purposes and a long tradition establishing the methods of different programs, but for many important public programs this is hardly the case. Instead, there is a sharp controversy about purposes and uncertainty about means. In a world in which the policies and programs are not "institutionalized," and the people who share the authority for setting the purposes are divided among themselves and keep changing, it is very difficult to establish terms of accountability that are compelling to public officials.

This point takes on added significance when one recognizes that the public sector has much more of one kind of incentive to distribute than the private sector. That special incentive is notoriety and public reputation. Government officials operate in a fishbowl.[24] Their actions are discussed in newspapers, radio, and TV and publicly praised or condemned. They are caricatured as good men making wise decisions and bringing common sense to government or as corrupt or inept men who find their simple duties well beyond their capacities. Their motives and backgrounds are closely scrutinized and publicly discussed.[25] To those who have never been subjected to this public review, the fuss may not seem anywhere nearly as powerful as increases or decreases in annual salary. But to those who have experienced the public attention, the satisfaction that comes from being publicly praised as a statesman or leader and the anxiety created by public condemnation feel every bit as powerful as the financial incentives wielded by private sector organizations. Indeed, since it is precisely the desire to gain virtue that often motivates people to serve in the public sector, public praise and blame are likely to mean more to them than to those who stay in the private domain.[26]

The problem with praise and blame as a mechanism of accountability is not that it is not powerful and not that there is insufficient variability in its allocation among officials. The basic problem is the *basis* on which it is allocated. If shifts in purposes, measurement, and leadership create uncertainty in the allocation of economic incentives (and thereby weaken their power as incentives and instruments of accountability), they have an even more devastating impact on the allocation of status incentives. The problem is that from the public official's point of view, press coverage and notoriety seem capricious. It is almost impossible to predict when the spotlight will be turned on and to guess whether it will reveal a noble civil servant or a goat. Moreover, it seems almost certain that a positive story in one newspaper will be followed by a negative one in another. In short, press coverage seems to follow its own logic, which is relatively independent of an official's actual performance.

In general, then, it is not that public officials face no sanctions for their performance. They *do* face economic sanctions. And even more important, they are often exposed to public praise or blame—a sanction that means a great deal to everyone, but particularly to those who choose to work in the government. The more fundamental problem is that the relationship between these sanctions and the terms of accountability is not firmly established, and this problem, in turn, is caused more by shifting mandates and leadership than the absence of powerful incentives.

Summary

For all of these reasons, accountability in government is a more complicated problem than it first appears. The mandated goals that define the valued characteristics of government programs are ambiguous, formulated at many different levels of abstraction, marked by continuing political conflict, and quite volatile. Measurement of performance against the goals is inherently difficult, yet little investment is made in the creation or maintenance of consistent systems of measurement. Since government often tries to act through other agencies in government or the private sector, and since these other organizations think of themselves as relatively independent with purposes of their own, the government's ability to make them accountable to it so that the government itself can be accountable to legislature is quite limited. There is an inherent tension between managing within simple notions of accountability and at the same time being flexible enough in operations to accommodate a wide variety of individual circumstances and to experiment with new ways of carrying out a program. And the financial and reputational incentives that motivate public managers to be effective are only imperfectly related to the substantive structure of accountability—that is, the agreements as to purposes and means of their efforts on behalf of the public.

Despite these difficulties, the pursuit of accountability remains an active and vital goal of our politics, which is as it should be. The important question, however, is exactly how we pursue accountability and whether the means chosen are appropriate to the realities of our current situation. That is the central question to be addressed in evaluating the investments we have made in Offices of Inspectors-General, for their primary justification is that they have or will enhance accountability in government in ways that will improve performance and restore public confidence in the government institutions.

Notes

[1] For a comprehensive view of the analytic literature relating to the problem of accountability in principal-agent relationships, see John W. Pratt and Richard J. Zeckhauser, "Principals and Agents," in John W. Pratt and Richard J. Zeckhauser, eds. *Principals and Agents: The Structure of Business* (Boston: Harvard Business School Press, 1985).

[2] This question of whether increased control increases or decreases the performance of organizations has been at the center of several decades of research and debate. Douglas MacGregor established the original terms of the debate between "Theory X" and "Theory Y." See *The Human Side of Enterprise* (New York: McGraw-Hill, 1960), chaps. 3 and 4. For more contemporary versions of the debate, see William Ouchi, *Theory Z: How American Business Can Meet the Japanese Challenge* (Reading, MA: Addison-Wesley, 1981); and Thomas J. Peters and Robert H. Waterman, *In Search of Excellence* (New York: Harper & Row, 1982), chap. 12.

[3] I am indebted to my colleague Walter Broadnax for emphasizing this point.

[4] Richard Elmore, "Models of Program Implementation," *Public Policy* 26 (Spring 1978): 185–228.

[5] We were surprised to discover that many private sector organizations that could design their control systems on the basis of revenues or profits nonetheless choose to design them on outputs since these give managers stronger incentives to do their particular jobs—namely, produce a product or deliver a service. The question of whether the product sells is a problem to be considered by top management less frequently. Thus, McDonald's and Burger King control their stores on physical characteristics such as length of wait in line, cleanliness of restrooms, cheerfulness of personnel rather than revenues earned or profits generated. See

"Burger King," Harvard University, Harvard Business School, Case #9-681-045, and the "McDonald Corporation," Harvard University, Harvard Business School, Case #9-681-044.

[6] See, for example, the testimony of Albert Angrisani, the Assistant Secretary for Employment and Training in the Department of Labor. "Without the work liability meaning something—without a prime sponsor knowing, for example, that in a very short . . . time, if a misspent fund is identified, that a prime sponsor is going to be responsible for it . . . [that] future funds will be offset, or their Charter will be revoked . . . —without that, we . . . will not be able to . . . make the word liability stick." Robert Leavitt, "The Inspector General at the Department of Labor," Harvard University, Kennedy School of Government, Case #C15-82-487, 1982.

[7] To a degree, GAO audits and reports may be understood as filling out the terms of broad charters established in authorization and appropriation bills. They do this by commenting on current performance and making recommendations for improvement in more particular and concrete terms than the general statutes.

[8] For general descriptions of the organization and performance of the U.S. Congress, see Norman J. Ornstein, ed., "Changing Congress: The Committee System," *Annals of the American Academy of Political and Social Science*, vol. 411 (1974); and Mark Green, *Who Runs Congress* (New York: Bantam Books, 1979).

[9] For an account of the relationships between political appointees and career civil servants, see Hugh Heclo, *A Government of Strangers* (Washington, DC: Brookings Institution, 1977).

[10] For an account of court interventions, see Donald Horowitz, *The Courts and Social Policy* (Washington, DC: Brookings Institution, 1977).

[11] For an account of the role of expert opinion in shaping and legitimating public policy, see Don K. Price, *The Scientific Estate* (Cambridge, MA: Harvard University Press, 1965).

[12] Peters and Waterman, *In Search of Excellence*, pp. 30–54.

[13] For an elaborate management system that rewards managers for investments as well as short-run operating performance, see "Texas Instruments: Management Systems," Harvard University, Harvard Business School, Case #172-054.

[14] Ibid., fn. 5.

[15] For a basic text on the evaluation of public sector activities, see Edward M. Gramlich, *Benefit Cost Analysis of Government Programs* (Englewood Cliffs, NJ: Prentice-Hall, 1981). For a basic text on program evaluation techniques, see Carol H. Weiss, *Evaluation Research: Methods for Assessing Program Effectiveness* (Englewood Cliffs, NJ: Prentice-Hall, 1972). For analyses of how much impact such studies have on decision-making in the public sector, see Laurence E. Lynn, ed. *Knowledge and Power: The Uncertain Connection* (Washington, DC: National Academy of Sciences, 1978).

[16] Mosher, "The Changing Responsibilities and Tactics of the Federal Government," *Public Administration Review* 40 (November-December 1980): 541–48.

[17] Bruce L. R. Smith and D. C. Hague, eds. *The Dilemma of Accountability in Modern Government: Independence v. Control* (New York: St. Martin's Press, 1971).

[18] Olivia A. Golden, "Management Without Control: Federal Managers and Local Service Delivery Under the Comprehensive Employment and Training Act,"

(unpublished doctoral dissertation, Harvard University, Kennedy School of Government, 1983).

[19] For an example, see "Life Safety Code," Boston University, School of Management, Case #9-378-925.

[20] Jerome T. Murphy and David K. Cohen, "Accountability in Education—The Michigan Experience," *Public Interest*, no. 36 (Summer 1974):53–81.

[21] Herbert Kaufmann, *Red Tape: Its Origins, Uses and Abuses* (Washington, DC: Brookings Institution, 1977).

[22] This situation has been changed to a degree by the 1978 Civil Service Reform Act, which gives federal managers much more discretion in assigning and rewarding senior career executives. For a discussion, see James W. Singer, "Changing the Guard: Reagan's Chance to Remold the Bureaucracy," *National Journal*, November 29, 1980, pp. 2028–31.

[23] Heclo, *Government of Strangers*, p. 104.

[24] Michael Blumenthal, "Candid Reflections of a Businessman in Washington," *Fortune*, January 29, 1979, pp. 36–49.

[25] Financial disclosure laws have added to these burdens. For a discussion of the privacy rights of public officials, see Dennis F. Thompson, "The Private Lives of Public Officials," in Joel L. Fleishman, Lance Leibman, and Mark Moore, eds., *Public Duties* (Cambridge, MA: Harvard University Press, 1981).

[26] For a discussion of these sorts of incentives, see James Q. Wilson, *Political Organizations* (New York: Basic Books, 1974).

Appendix B The Impact of the Offices of Inspectors-General on Program Operations

DEPARTMENT OF AGRICULTURE

Food Stamp Program
1. Reduced errors in eligibility and benefit determination:
   a. Created liability for negligent issuance of stamps; recipients must present photo in cities of 100,000 inhabitants
   b. Required use of social security number for identification of clients
   c. Used "computer matches" more frequently to check on accuracy of claimants' statements
   d. Reduced use of "expedited service"
   e. Established faster administrative process to recover small losses from clients
   f. Expanded federal administrative support to state efforts to control fraud, abuse, and waste
2. Reduced losses/thefts/fraud associated with distribution of authorizations to purchase stamps and stamps themselves:
   a. Created serial numbers on stamps to aid investigations of diverted stamps
   b. Eliminated block purchase requirements (which makes

stamps more accessible to people and reduces number in circulation)

    c. Developed "secure issuance" systems for "authorizations to purchase": registered mail, time limits on ATP's

    d. Used aggressive investigative techniques against large food stamp traffickers

    e. Eliminated wholesaler redemption of food stamps to prevent large-scale trafficking

3. Improved cash management: Required that stamp issuers pay Treasury more promptly for stamps

Farmer's Home Administration: Emergency Loan Program

1. Reduced errors in eligibility and benefit determination:
    a. Required that claimants have sustained (30%) physical losses (both amount and shift to physical rather than financial losses represent tightening)
    b. Required that claimants pledge all assets in seeking credit elsewhere and in claiming credit from government
    c. Made more rigorous tests for claimants' inability to claim credit elsewhere (actual turndowns; verification by FmHA)

2. Minimized period of government financial exposure: Expedited earlier and more frequent "graduation reviews" to shift loans to commercial sources

Farmer's Home Administration: Business and Industrial Loan Program

1. Eliminated "political influence" in making large guaranteed loans:
    a. Specified in detail procedure for reviewing loan applications at each level; required that both local and top level recommendations be written
    b. Documented all contacts of high-level officials with interested parties

2. Reduced errors in eligibility determination and magnitude of government support:
    a. Urged improved technical reviews of financial position of applicant and financial and technical feasibility of proposed projects
    b. Urged that creditor hold at least 10% equity in enterprise
    c. To protect government, urged assurance that other par-

ties to deal have liability and capacity to pay before government
d. Put ceilings on size of loan guarantees established
3. Overall Cut in Program
4. Existing Management Removed

DEPARTMENT OF LABOR

Comprehensive Employment and Training Act Program

1. Closed audit gap: Required that "prime sponsors" procure own audit every year if OIG cannot perform
2. Expedited process of audit resolution:
   a. Agreed on how to handle cost items that were holding up resolutions in many areas (e.g., time and attendance records for PSE employees, refreshment costs for administrative meetings, officer travel, on-the-job training incremental costs to employees, line-item overexpenditures)
   b. Established IG sign-off requirement to close audit
   c. Required that high-level management pay attention to close audits, including prereview of resolutions in which program officer allows "questioned costs"
3. Exerted stronger pressure on debt collection:
   a. Required that interest charges on debts owed to federal government start 30 days after audit resolution regardless of whether findings are appealed to Administrative Law Judge
   b. Assigned personal responsibility to regional directors for debt collection goals
   c. Asked for cash recoveries from states for debts rather than in-kind contributions or service at no cost to government
4. Had limited success with investigation of fraud:
   a. Most fraud was by program managers wanting to claim more performance than actually achieved
   b. Investigations sometimes interfered with administrative efforts to solve problems since suspects and existing procedures were left in place during investigations
   c. Investigations were reactive; investigators thought greater chance for success in prevention
5. Phased out PSE program

Federal Employees Compensation Act Program
1. Reduced errors in eligibility and benefit determination:
   a. Created new forms that placed responsibility and liability on claimants to report accurate and timely information about status
   b. Established and utilized "profile" of "high-risk" FECA claimants to target computer matches and investigations (pilot program to use in half of office)
   c. Pressured to provide more complete documentation of determination made in case files and to install ADP capabilities to assist in checking adequacy of files
2. Reduced provider fraud:
   a. Established FECA authority to bar providers who have defrauded government from continuing to participate
   b. Pressured to check and validate provider claims
   c. Pressured (strongly resisted) to establish "fee schedule" for payments